SINAI

SUMMIT
Meeting God with
Our Character Crisis

SINAI
SUMMIT
Meeting God with
Our Character Crisis

cᴑ

RICK ATCHLEY

— A —
FAITH FOCUS
Book

Sweet Publishing

Fort Worth, Texas

Sinai Summit
Meeting God with Our Character Crisis

Copyright © 1993 by Sweet Publishing,
Fort Worth, TX 76137

Library of Congress Catalog Number 92-63189

ISBN: 0-8344-0228-9

Printed in the U. S. A.
10 9 8 7 6 5 4 3 2

This book is lovingly dedicated to
my wife Jamie.
Her help made this work possible.
Her example lets me know a life of character
is possible, too.

Contents

Introduction

God's principles are eternal because "God is the same yesterday, today, and forever." What he said in the past is true for today and will be true for the future. His principles for developing strong character in his people are no different. They were true for our spiritual ancestors at Mount Sinai, they are true for us today in America, and they will be true for our descendants around the world.

Unfortunately, through the years, we have seen God's eternal principles for living lives of character as negative commands. "Don't do this. . ." and "don't do that. . . ." Many people have turned away from God's principles, thinking them to be pessimistic "downers" and unworkable in an upbeat, contemporary society.

But wait! If the negative side of a principle is true, the positive side of that principle must also be true. This book will help you focus on the positive side of God's principles for character building and happy living. For instance, God's instruction, "Don't put any other gods before me," which sounds negative, can be stated in the positive: "Put God first." Or, "Don't make idols for yourselves," can easily be stated "Keep 'things' in perspective." Looking at his principles from the positive viewpoint suddenly puts them in a whole new light and gives us insight into God's underlying good intentions for his children. It's an exciting and joyous discovery!

Jesus himself restated God's eternal principles for character building while he was on earth, either in words or by his example. He certainly recognized their validity in his society, which was more contemporary than that of the Hebrews at Mount Sinai.

And while we believe our society is more contemporary than that of Jesus, we must also recognize that God's omnipotence allowed him to structure principles that are timeless and valuable for all ages.

If you think God's eternal principles for living lives of character are out of date, think again. They are no more out of date than God himself. They are "new every morning." His ten principles are no more out of date than his grace, his mercy, and his salvation. They are, in fact, the key to a life of integrity and happiness for you and your family.

Come with us to the Sinai Summit. Come meet with God!

The Publisher

Exodus 20 *And God spoke all these words:*

²*"I am the LORD your God, who brought you out of Egypt, out of the land of slavery.*

³*"You shall have no other gods before me.*

⁴*"You shall not make for yourself an idol in the form of anything in heaven above or on the earth beneath or in the waters below. ⁵You shall not bow down to them or worship them; for I, the LORD your God, am a jealous God, punishing the children for the sin of the fathers to the third and fourth generation of those who hate me, ⁶but showing love to a thousand generations of those who love me and keep my commandments.*

⁷*"You shall not misuse the name of the LORD your God, for the LORD will not hold anyone guiltless who misuses his name.*

⁸*"Remember the Sabbath day by keeping it holy. ⁹Six days you shall labor and do all your work, ¹⁰but the seventh day is a Sabbath to the LORD your God. On it you shall not do any work, neither you, nor your son or daughter, nor your manservant or maidservant, nor your animals, nor the alien within your gates. ¹¹For in six days the LORD made the heavens and the earth, the sea, and all that is in them, but he rested on the seventh day. Therefore the LORD blessed the Sabbath day and made it holy.*

¹²*"Honor your father and your mother, so that you may live long in the land the LORD your God is giving you.*

¹³*"You shall not murder.*

¹⁴*"You shall not commit adultery.*

¹⁵*"You shall not steal.*

¹⁶*"You shall not give false testimony against your neighbor.*

¹⁷*"You shall not covet your neighbor's house. You shall not covet your neighbor's wife, or his manservant or maidservant, his ox or donkey, or anything that belongs to your neighbor."*

Chapter 1

Down from the Mountain

∾

T he conference site was shrouded in thick, dark clouds. Held in a secluded place at the peak of a mountain in the desert, the Sinai Summit was both highly secret and top-level. Security was extremely tight. No one was allowed above the base of the mountain itself, except one ambassador. Anyone who crossed the barrier would be killed instantly.

> ***The Quest for Character***
>
> *Exodus 19—34*
> *Galatians 5:13-23*

The conference had convened weeks before. The people waiting for the outcome were becoming nervous and worried. Only a couple of times had the ambassador emerged from the summit to make sketchy reports and give clipped instructions. Then he had returned to the mountain peak to await the results.

Issues on the conference table to be resolved were of global proportion. The result of the meeting would mean either long-term security and communal well-being or the decay and eventual destruction of the nation. It was critical that solutions be reached for the common good.

At long last, the great statesman and ambassador was seen coming down from the mountain. His face was shining. His step was lighter than before. And under his arm was evidence of the covenant terms involving the two parties. The people gathered around the base of the mountain to hear the reading of the agreement and treaty.

Every person would be invited to come to the mountain peak to accept the Code of Ethics personally.

Clearing his throat, the aging ambassador announced that the Sinai Summit had, indeed, been an unprecedented success. The great Power over heaven and earth had formulated an everlasting Code of Ethics which would both guide the people and save them from destruction. This Code of Ethics contained ten principles which, if endorsed and accepted by each generation, would ensure a nation of pure character and, thus, leadership among men and favor with God.

Acceptance of the covenant, however, was to be by voluntary compliance only. No person or nation would be coerced by a military force or other enforcement agency to accept or live by its principles. The people would accept or reject it on an individual basis, recognizing its great personal benefits or accepting the inevitable consequences for ignoring the instructions.

In a final sweeping move, the great Power had agreed to keep the Sinai Summit in session for all time so that every person and every generation would be assured of the validity and timelessness of these values.

Then came the crowning announcement: Every person would be invited to come to the mountain peak to accept the Code of Ethics personally. And each person who accepted the covenant would be granted the supreme blessing of unwavering character and purity of life—moral excellence.

The ambassador showed the people the great document. It bore the seal of the one and only God of Heaven, Lord of lords, King of kings, and Lord of heaven's armies.

Looking out at the people, the old ambassador's eyes were bright with happy tears. His smile was warm, and his love for the people was evident. Carrying the document, he walked slowly through the silent people to his tent. Then he turned and quietly said, "Now it's up to you." Then he went into his tent to await the people's response.

The Response

For generation after generation, people have been responding to God's Code of Ethics. Some have responded positively; some have responded negatively. And now it's our turn to respond . . . as individuals and as a nation. In fact, the need to return to the Sinai Summit has never been greater in our land.

America's Character Crisis

Today America is being threatened by a crisis. It's not an economic crisis. It's not a foreign threat. It's not related to the environment, either. We seldom hear the word "crisis" associated with this danger; in fact, the threat is seldom recognized as such. But it's here. We read about it in the newspaper in articles about financial advisors embezzling money from the clients who for years have trusted them. We see it in TV news reports about teenagers who kill elderly people for the "thrill" of watching someone die. We hear about it from our schools when we discover a child has been beaten up physically or emotionally by his peers because he looks different from most of the kids at his school. What is this threat to our society? My friends, **America is facing a crisis of failed character**. That's right. America's greatest deficit today is a deficit of character.

America has, as a whole, rejected the Code of Ethics presented at the Sinai Summit. This message will not be popular with most in our society. Many would scoff at anyone expressing much concern over our predicament. Indeed, as a society, we are a lot like the guy who jumped off a 100-story building. About 50 stories down, a lady stuck her head out a window and asked, "How's it going?" and the guy replied, "So far, so good." Things may seem fine in the midst of the fall, but that man is headed for a deadly crash. And so is America, if we don't somehow manage to stop the free-fall of our character.

Role Models

The task before us is an awesome one. Where can we look today for models of character? To our statesmen and stateswomen? Every week our newspapers and magazines tell us about a new scandal in

Washington. Every president in recent memory, for instance, has been the subject of books disclosing "skeletons in the closet." Much of the debate in the 1992 presidential campaign centered on the question of which candidate's character most *dis*qualified him to be president. This generation has even seen a president of the United States forced to resign from office to avoid impeachment because of his lies and lack of ethical standards.

If we cannot look to leaders in government for models of character, then can we look to heads of industry? Here, too, we see a deplorable lack of character. One headline after another screams at us about strongholds of American industry being convicted of tax evasion, fraud, insider trading, sexual harrassment, etc.

Saddest of all, we cannot even look to what the world considers religious leaders for examples of character. Over the last few years we have seen nationally recognized individuals claiming to represent Christ forced out of their pulpits for sexual sins, sent to prison for fraud, and exposed as charlatans and crooks on national television.

The Facts

It is no wonder, then, in light of the character (or lack thereof) of America's leaders that individuals in our country are exhibiting a lack of character as well. You know the crime statistics, but let me remind you: a serious crime is committed every two seconds in this country. A rape is committed every six minutes. A murder every twenty-three minutes.

Our lack of character, of moral standing, is not just evidenced by crime rates, however. Many of us who would never consider committing a violent crime see no problem with "being creative" on our income taxes or with padding our résumés.

We see nothing wrong with working ourselves into an early grave in order to accumulate wealth and prestige. On the contrary, our materialistic society lauds workaholism as a virtue. Meanwhile, spouses, children, parents—all those nearest to us—are seeking counsel, therapy, or perhaps divorce because they can't understand how we can love them and still neglect them so completely.

Indeed, the term "family commitment" has lost much of its meaning to our society. Not only have we too often made family members take a back seat to personal ambition, but in doing so, we've taught a whole new generation the concept of "disposable family." In 1990, for the first time in our country's history, over 50 percent of American high school seniors said they did not expect to marry one person and stay in that marriage for a lifetime.

It seems there are a lot of disillusioned people out there. We've seen the most prominent leaders in our country throw away the standards and principles we were brought up to accept, and we are raising a new generation of selfish young people that is not only very cynical, but is more morally indifferent than ever before. Not only do they not know if anything is wrong, they do not really care.

Absolute or Obsolete?

What do you think of when you hear the term "the Ten Commandments"? For some of us, it summons up childhood days in Sunday school and memory work for recitation. For some, it symbolizes a list of rules carved in stone "back before God became a Christian." And, if the truth be known, for others the "Ten Commandments" conjures up nothing more concrete than the image of Charleton Heston and a cast of thousands.

For most of us, the "Ten Commandments" is a term we have heard and used since childhood. But a recent *Newsweek* survey found that only 49 percent of Protestants and 44 percent of Catholics in this country could name even four of those commandments. Why such ignorance in the face of seeming familiarity? Could it be we think we've outgrown the Ten Commandments? Are they merely simpler rules for simpler times? In other words, is God's Code of Ethics—his Ten Commandments—absolute or obsolete? The apostle Paul knew them to be timeless values (Galatians 5:13-23) that can guide us through the moral wilderness of our day just as dependably as the God who authored them led the children of Israel through the wilderness to the promised land almost 3,500 years ago. The real need of America is the discovery, or perhaps I should say the recovery, of an ethical creed that can provide constant moral guidance for America. And that's how we come to the Ten Commandments—the Code of Ethics. They are not obsolete. In fact, nothing short of a return to their principles will suffice. Lip service simply will not do. Ted Koppel laid out the challenge for us at the Duke University commencement in May 1987 when he said,

> We have actually convinced ourselves that slogans will save us. Shoot up if you want, but use a clean needle. Enjoy sex whenever and with whomever you wish, but wear a condom.
>
> No. The answer is No. Not because it isn't cool or smart or because you might end up in jail or dying in an AIDS ward, but "no" because it's wrong, because we have spent 5,000 years as a race of rational human beings, trying to drag ourselves out of the primeval slime by searching

for truth and moral absolutes. . . .

Our society finds truth too strong a medicine to digest undiluted. In its purest form, truth is not a polite tap on the shoulder. It is a howling reproach. What Moses brought down from Mount Sinai were not the Ten Suggestions. They are commandments. Are, not were. The sheer brilliance of the Ten Commandments is that they codify in a handful of words accept-able human behavior, not just for then or now, but for all time.

For too long, our society has treated God's Code of Ethics like a president emeritus—like someone too old to be of practical use, but to be honored at cer-emonies and other "big" events. When we put aside his standards, of course, what we really do is "retire" God. This is his Code of Ethics. It started with him. So, maybe before we start studying the principles themselves, we need to do some background work.

Reasons for the Summit

The first step in understanding God's principles for living lives of character is to know the story behind the Summit. It's a story of a world that was stalling, a world that was heading nowhere, hurting each other, hating each other—a world that had come to listen to Satan's lies so completely that it didn't even recognize the voice of God. Out of this world God chose a man—Abraham—and said, "Through you I'm going to win the world back and teach them how to live." God made this man a pil-grim and a father. God gave him a place to live, a land he promised to this pilgrim's descendants. Later, those descendants left that land of promise and went down to Egypt. They stayed there for 400

years and were made slaves. They endured cruelty
and hardship. But God had mercy on them in their
misery, so he sent a deliverer named Moses to re-
deem these people. Through a series of miracles, God
delivered these people from their cruel bondage and
brought them out of Egypt to a place called Sinai.
And it was there, at Sinai, God wrote in stone this
Code of Ethics—his guide for valued, empowered
living.

---

*God wrote in stone this Code of Ethics—
his guide for valued, empowered living.*

The reason it's important to remember this story
is that to understand God's ethics, we must view
them against this backdrop of liberation. God did not
deliver these guidelines so that his people would feel
burdened or restricted. In fact, the first thing he said
was, "I am the LORD your God, who brought you out
of Egypt, out of the land of slavery." God did not
bring Israel out of slavery so that he could make
them slaves all over again; he brought them out of
slavery so that they could be free. And he gave them
these principles for living so that they would know
how to live freely. And he gave them to us also so
that we could know how to live freely—how to live
lives of character.

Not all limits bind. I give my children limits. I tell
them not to tease and make fun of others. Do I want
to take away their freedom to express themselves?
No. I just want our family environment to be a place
where people feel safe and loved. I also tell them not
to eat food they find on the ground. Do I want my
children to starve? No. I want them to be safe so
they can enjoy food for the rest of their lives. I don't

give my children guidelines because I want to make them slaves, but because I want them to live happy and free lives. God wants the same for his children.

We've called his plan the Ten Commandments, and, in a way, that's a suitable name. But through the years, some have come to believe that these are just arbitrary dictates from on high. They sometimes make the mistake of thinking God's Code of Ethics was barked down by some staff sergeant up in heaven trying to trip them up. But the people who first heard these instructions did not make this error. The Jews called God's plan the "Ten Words." They also called it *Torah*, which simply means "instruction." And perhaps these names are more meaningful, for instruction for living is exactly what God intended his words to be. Rather than thinking of the Ten Commandments as a list of rules, we should think of them as our Father's teaching and instruction.

The Jews called God's plan the "Ten Words."

When we study God's Code of Ethics, we should look at them as though we are with our Heavenly Father, needing guidance about what to do or how to understand the world. And he puts his hand on our shoulder and says, "Listen, my child, life works better like this . . ." Every single instruction teaches us something of what is necessary to live as a community that pleases God and honors him and the people in it. That is why God told his people, "Follow them so that you may live. . . . Observe them carefully, for this will show your wisdom and understanding to the nations" (Deuteronomy 4:1, 6). God said if you build your lives and your communities by these values, the other nations will look at you and say, "There goes a wise and understanding people. We should structure our society like theirs because what they do works." It's a relevant ethic for any time and any culture anywhere. You never get too old, too sophisticated, too mature for God's instruction.

The wisest man who ever lived, King Solomon, summed it up this way: "Here is my final advice: Honor God and obey his commands. This is the most important thing people can do" (Ecclesiastes 12:13, NCV). Living God's way makes life full; it makes life complete; it brings wholeness to a people.

Solomon's words make me think of a conversation I read in a magazine recently. A news reporter was interviewing a homeowner in southern Florida just after Hurricane Andrew had devastated the area. This particular man's home was the only one in the neighborhood still standing after the storm. When questioned by the reporter, the man replied, "I built this house myself, and I made sure that I followed all the state building codes. These other builders tried to cut corners to save a few dollars, and look what happened. If they had just followed the code, these homes would still be standing."

The greatest problem in America today is the character deficit. And the greatest need is to find an ethical code that will guide, sustain, and enrich us in any and every circumstance—an absolute value system on which we can build our lives and our communities. I realize some will disagree with my assessment of our situation. But let me encourage those of you who do agree to accompany me on a journey. A pilgrimage in quest of character. A return to the Sinai Summit.

Focusing Your Faith

1. Imagine that you are among God's people at the base of Mount Sinai waiting for the results of the Sinai Summit. Describe the feelings you experience when you see Moses coming down the mountain with the Code of Ethics.

2. How many principles of the Ten Commandments—God's Code of Ethics—can you name without looking?

3. Read Exodus 20:1-17. Pray for understanding of this passage. In what ways do God's Code of Ethics give you freedom and happiness?

4. When was the last time the Father gently "put his hand on your shoulder" and said, "Life works better like this . . ."? What principle had you been ignoring?

5. What is your church doing that will cause people in your town to say, "There goes a wise and understanding people"?

6. In your opinion, what is the biggest cause of today's character crisis?

7. Why do you think many today view the Bible and the church as no longer relevant?

Chapter 2

For Moses' Time or All Time?

✂

In the fall of 1968, President Lyndon Johnson made a visit to former President Harry S. Truman's home in Independence, Missouri.

> **The Character Deficit**
>
> *Genesis 2 and 3*
> *Mark 7:21-23*

"Harry," Johnson said, "you and Bess are getting on in years. You ought to have an army medical corpsman living with you in this big, old house."

"Really, Lyndon, can I have that?" Truman asked.

"Of course you can, Harry. You're an ex-president of the United States. I'll arrange it," Johnson replied. And he did arrange it.

After LBJ left the White House in 1969, a reporter caught up with him one day close to the Pedernales River near his home in Texas. The reporter thought he had discovered a chink in Johnson's armor and political ethic.

"Is it true that you have an army medical corpsman living here on the ranch with you?" asked the reporter.

"Of course, it's true," Johnson said. "After all, Harry Truman has one."

That's how one improper act leads to another. That's how America and the world got into this mess. One moral slide led to another, and then to another, and now we're nearing the bottom of the pit.

> *One moral slide led to another, and then to another, and now we're nearing the bottom of the pit.*

Jacob Riis, a well-known social reformer, once commented, "When nothing seems to help, I go and look at a stonecutter hammering away at his rock perhaps a hundred times without as much as a crack showing in it. Yet, at the hundred and first blow, it will split in two, and I know it was not that specific blow that did it—but all that had gone before."

Every immoral act is another blow against God's Code of Ethics. Every lie is another tear in its fabric. Every act of envy is an unmendable rip. And when will the raveling stop? Will there be any part of the garment still intact when the Lord returns?

John Steinbeck, in his book *Of Mice and Men,* pointed out the decline in moral values when one of his characters commented, "There's nothing *wrong* anymore." And that seems to be the atmosphere today in America. Nothing is *wrong* anymore. Adultery isn't wrong. Lying isn't wrong. Abortion isn't wrong. Homosexuality isn't wrong. Materialism isn't wrong. Idolatry toward money isn't wrong. Divorce and family abandonment aren't even wrong.

People today agree that the moral climate is deteriorating and that something must be done about it. The problem is that too many people don't know what it takes to create a moral America. They're writing their own definitions for morals rather than looking to God's special instructions for help.

Where Did It All Start?

To understand the roots of our character crisis, we must go all the way back to the Garden of Eden in Genesis 2 and 3. God had just finished the creation of the world, and the masterpieces among all creation are the beings called "man." God placed these people in charge of all creation, and he gave them all they needed for a bountiful life. They truly lived a miraculous existence, for, in all their labor, the earth cooperated with them. God gave them the fruit of any tree for their food; however, he said, "You must not eat from the tree of the knowledge of good and evil, for when you eat of it you will surely die" (Genesis 2:17). The people lived in accordance with God's instructions, and, as he surveyed all his handiwork, he put his stamp of approval on it all: "It is very good."

It was good because God was at the center of all creation. He is the definition of good, you see. Anything consistent with God is good. Anything that is not consistent with God is evil. God was the only standard of ethics available to Adam and Eve, but it was a flawless one.

Suddenly, onto the scene came Satan. He convinced the people that God wasn't as powerful as

they had thought ("You will not surely die," Genesis
3:4); that he wasn't as loving as he would like them
to believe (God's prohibiting the fruit was simply
meant to deny them some pleasure); and that God
didn't *have* to be the standard of right and wrong
("God knows that when you eat of it your eyes will be
opened, and you will be like God, knowing good and
evil," Genesis 3:5).

From the first bite of that fruit, people began a
moral decline that is continuing today, fueled by our
stubborn determination to define good and evil by
what is consistent with *our* will, not *God's*. Unfortunately, we simply aren't made to handle that kind of
load. Throughout religious and secular history, we
see the tragic effects of this kind of thinking. Indeed,
measuring morality by our own standards is the
birth of all thinking such as "the ends justify the
means," "might makes right," and any other
catchphrases that we've used through the ages to
rationalize the cruel and selfish goals we've pursued.

Every Person for Himself

We've had character problems for a long, long
time—ask Noah. But what is truly alarming is that
in modern times we are approaching the logical end
of an every-person-for-himself system of defining
morality. We've almost completely lost a shared
understanding of what is right. We're not just breaking laws in America anymore; we are denying that
anybody has a right to make laws. The only absolute
is that everything, including ethics, is relative. And
the result of this philosophical free-for-all is the
wave of permissiveness in which our society is
drowning.

Consider for a minute the thinking we're being
asked to accept. Today, we are told, there are no

absolutes—no rights or wrongs for all times and situations. Instead, we must decide in any given circumstance what is right or wrong for that specific situation. Doesn't that sound good? After all, each situation is different.

But this ethic overestimates our ability to choose what is right, and what we end up with, at best, is "enlightened" self-interest. The way this ethic tends to work is that "what is right is what I want." Ernest Hemingway's statement quoted in a 1970's _Newsweek_ article entitled "The Second Sexual Revolution" sums up this philosophy quite bluntly. Hemingway says, "What is moral is what I feel good after, and what is immoral is what I feel bad after." In other words, if I want it, if I like it, if it makes me feel good, it's right, because I am the moral center of my universe. Of course, what is good for me may not be good for you, but those are the breaks. Just don't impose your standards on me.

We're not just breaking laws in America anymore; we are denying that anybody has a right to make laws.

Everyone has been "doing what is right in his own eyes" (Judges 17:6, NASB). This every-person-for-himself idea has crept into almost every facet of our thinking. It helps explain why we choose entertainment—whether TV, movies, or books where we find ourselves hoping the leading characters "get together" whether or not they are married to each other (or to someone else). It explains why in many shows today the "bad guys" are the heroes. After all, they're just "marching to the beat of a different drummer."

This every-person-for-himself thinking is also clearly central to the current debate over the work of certain recording artists and their First Amendment rights. You may not know (though you need to) that within a recent twelve-month span, one recording artist released a song in which she suggests that little girls like to be tied up and spanked. Another released a song in which he glorifies the wonders of incest. And one rap group released an album that is blatant in its glory of violence committed on women during sexual intercourse.

When people who don't buy into this thinking stand up and say that these kinds of lyrics are wrong, the social commentators who guard the conscience of America lash back and sloganize, "Artistic freedom!". . . "First Amendment rights!". . . "Down with censorship!" They try to conjure up images of puritanism or book-burning, and they suggest that their type of entertainment is thought-provoking, challenging, and avant-garde. But what I see, instead, is a nation committing moral "suicide" under the name of sophistication. Indeed, the Bible says, "There is a way that seems right to a man, but in the end it leads to death" (Proverbs 14:12).

---

*"We need more people who stand up
and say to people in school, that
character is important."*

General H. Norman Schwarzkopf, who led America's triumph over Sadam Hussein in the Gulf War, agrees. In an interview with the editor of the History Book Club in the fall of 1992, Schwarzkopf said, "What I would like to see in our school system, military and civilian, [when talking about] leadership

is to emphasize the importance of character, the
importance of ethics, and the importance of morality.
We need more people who stand up and say to
people in school, particularly high school and college
students, that character is important. Don't ignore
it."

Character is important. And the quest for character will be frustrated as long as we continue to use
ourselves as the standard for right and wrong. That
is why we need to return to the Sinai Summit.
There, as we encounter the holy presence of God, we
begin to understand that he alone is the moral
center. God is the only eternal standard of good, the
only source of real values. And in his instruction to
Moses we find the ethic we need to become people of
character.

Let's consider in more detail why God's values are
the answer to America's character deficit.

The Right to Justice

God's Code of Ethics declares the right of all
people to experience justice. God values all people
equally. When God blesses the principle of rest one
day a week, for example, he says it is to be a blessing, not just for the wealthy, but for all people. He
says, "On it you shall not do any work, neither you,
nor your son or daughter, nor your manservant or
maidservant, nor your animals, nor the alien within
your gates" (Exodus 20:10b).

God's plan for character is unlike anything man
had developed in all of history. Several civilizations
had developed legal codes prior to or contemporary
with the Ten Commandments, but what distin-
guishes these rules for living from the others is that
the other codes' basic intent was to protect property.
In other words, the other codes were developed to

ensure that the people who had a lot of stuff kept it. In contrast, the essence of God's plan is not property, but people. God's words proclaim that people are what matter to him. God's plan is for people of character to be protectors of people, no matter how much money they have, what color or sex they are, or even how old they are. All people are made in his image, and people of character show respect for his image by respecting those made in it.

The Way to Love

God's Code of Ethics declares the way for all people to practice love. The Beatles were right years ago, when they said, "All you need is love." But the question we're left with is, what does that mean? How do we love each other? It is interesting that the apostle Paul said in Romans 13, "The commandments, 'Do not commit adultery,' 'Do not murder,' 'Do not steal,' 'Do not covet,' and whatever other commandments there may be, are summed up in this one rule: 'Love your neighbor as yourself.' "

God's ethic teaches us how to love. But the mistake many of us make is thinking that God wants us to be passively good. In other words, we think, "Okay, I'll just sit on my hands over here in my corner, and I won't kill or steal, and I'll be living by his standards." But that is not the ethic God desires at all.

When God says, "You shall not kill," he means for us to respect human life, to protect it. So, a person of character helps people who are homeless. And a person of character acts to protect victims of domestic abuse and violence. The principle is to love people by preserving and bettering their lives.

God also says, "Don't commit adultery." What this means is that God wants us to keep our covenants sacred. Marriage is sacred, a precious covenant with one other person that lasts for a lifetime. But when we break vows, someone—maybe our partner, maybe our mate, maybe our children, always ourself—gets hurt. So God says keeping sex sacred helps us behave as people of character in a sex-saturated world.

When God says, "Do not steal," what he means is "Keep 'things' in perspective." How many people are getting hurt today because materialism is rampant in our culture? We think if we could just have more, buy more, make more, we'd be happy. We may have to climb over the people in front of us to get the things we want, or leave behind the people who can't help us get them. But we're willing to pay the price, because we think getting "things" will make us happy.

God's ethic teaches us how to love.

But God's values stand in opposition to popular wisdom. He wants us to know that we can't find life by clawing and grabbing and cheating to get ahead. It's wrong to hurt people to get things. Jesus identified the intent of God's values long ago when a lawyer came to Jesus and asked him to sum up what God expected of people. Jesus replied that if we love God completely with passion, and if we love those around us as we love ourselves, we are living as God intended (Matthew 22:35-40). We are being what he designed and created us to be from the beginning. So, God's values teach us how to love.

The Need for Change

God's Code of Ethics declares the need of all people for inner change. Please don't make the mistake of thinking that all God is concerned about is external actions. Certainly, God's ethics deal with external actions, but he has always been most concerned with the heart, because it is from there that our actions come. As Jesus pointed out, we break the commandments in our heart before we ever break them with our hands or mouths: "For from within, out of men's hearts, come evil thoughts, sexual immorality, theft, murder, adultery, greed, malice, deceit, lewdness, envy, slander, arrogance and folly. All these evils come from inside and make a man 'unclean' " (Mark 7:21-23).

If we are to live lives that honor God and respect others, putting on a little behavioral makeup will not do. We must change from the inside out.

God is certainly not concerned with merely regulating our outward behavior. His ethic is not a rigid code of rules which we can obey only with our bodies, but loving principles we can honor in our hearts. Indeed, this call for inner obedience separates God's code from all others. Take the last instruction, for example. "You shall not covet." I don't have to physically do a thing to violate this part of God's plan. Coveting is an internal sin, but it leads to many external actions: stealing, lying, adultery, even murder. God wants us to see clearly that in reality all moral failure is an inner failure, for the heart is the battleground for Satan's spiritual assaults. If we are to live lives that honor God and respect others, putting on a little behavioral makeup will not do. We must change from the inside out.

We've seen, then, the desperate need in our society

for moral character—the kind only changeless values can produce. We've also seen that God has given us his Code of Ethics to fill this need, not just for Moses' time, or for our time, but for all time.

God intended his plan to liberate us from the forces that would enslave us. On one level, God was giving the children of Israel guidelines for how to live with character after leaving a land of slavery and in preparation for entering a land populated by people who would love to overpower and enslave them again. But on a much deeper level, he was giving his children for all times empowerment to remain free in a world where Satan is trying desperately to enslave their souls; for the Bible is clear that the problems resulting from our failure of character are, at their most basic level, the scars of spiritual warfare.

The character deficit began in Eden. But the Bible has good news for a world that has lost its character. God knows how to recharacter human beings. He has a gift called forgiveness that, through Christ, enables us to "start over" in our relationship with him. He has a power called the Holy Spirit which he gives us when we surrender completely to Christ. It is this Spirit that empowers us to live by his values in a world that has none.

***The Bible has good news for a world
that has lost its character.***

And now it's up to you. God can undo the damage of Eden, but only as you decide to make him and not self the moral center of life. You must climb to the summit and face God with your decisions to accept or reject his Code of Ethics for your life.

Focusing Your Faith

1. What is the most important value you learned as a child?

2. From watching you, what value do you think your children will learn (have learned)? What do you wish they would learn from you?

3. "We've almost completely lost a shared understanding of what is right." Give an example of people defining good and evil using themselves and not God as the standard.

4. Do you think Americans are simply ignoring God's principles or do they just interpret them differently today? Why?

5. Give an example that illustrates that the battle for values going on today is really a spiritual struggle.

6. If changing on the outside means changing on the inside first, what is the first step you must take to be recharactered?

7. What can your church do to help America out of this moral mess? What can you do?

Chapter 3

No Place but First Place

∽

When our son Michael was five and our daughter Morgan was almost three, we decided to teach them one of the principles of God's Code of Ethics each week. Night after night, I would go over the Exodus story with

> **Principle 1:**
>
> *Put God First*
>
> *Exodus 20:1-3*
> *Mark 12:28-30*

the kids, and then I'd try to teach them the "commandment of the week." After a few weeks, I thought I would test our system to see how well they were remembering "God's Rules," as we called them. So I asked the kids what rules they could remember. Michael did pretty well, and I was feeling pretty good about my teaching until Morgan's turn.

"Morgan," I said, "what rules do you remember?"
Morgan thought about it for a few minutes, then

replied, "Don't chew on tings."

"Okay," I said, "That's a pretty good rule. But can you remember any of *God's* rules?"

She pondered the question again, and said, "Don't wite on de walls."

Humbled, but not defeated, I put my teacher's ego on the line once more and said, "Those are good rules, Honey, but can you think of any of God's rules—the ones we've been talking about?"

She screwed up her face, deep in thought. Suddenly, a light came on! Hello! Contact! She pulled herself up to her full thirty-six inches of height and announced proudly, "Put your gum in de twash!"

Well, since then we have made some progress in communicating God's principles to our daughter. And now, when asked, the first one she names is invariably, "No udder gods." And really, that's the only place you can start. Put God first. No other gods.

Key to Character

The first key to building a life of character is this: Put God first! Now, most people today would probably be puzzled at our starting point. The world's prevailing attitude about character is that it has to do strictly with how a person handles his relationships with others, and that his religious beliefs are sort of an ethical side dish. They may add flavor to the main course, but they aren't essential to it. In fact, a few years ago, some university professors gave out copies of the Ten Commandments to their students and asked them to arrange them in order of importance. Ninety percent of the students reversed the order, putting the commandments about how we are to treat our fellow man first and the commandments about how we are to relate to God last.

Jesus himself clarified that issue when he said that the most important principle is to love God completely; and secondly, to love our neighbors (Mark 12:28-30). The Jews, however, understood the fact that the first four principles—those dealing with our relationship with God—provide the theological basis for living a life of character. In other words, they provide the _why_ for our living lives that so dramatically go against the current of our society.

This reversal of priorities is further evidence of Satan's success in convincing us that we can be the moral centers of our universe, and unbelievers are by no means the only people to fall prey to his deception. Look, for example, at the way we in the church have taught sexual morality. We have tried to convince people to abstain from sexual activity before marriage, which is certainly part of God's plan; but what reasons do we give people for obeying? The reasons I heard for abstaining when I was single were (1) If you don't, you might lose your reputation; (2) If you don't, you might get a disease; and (3) If you don't, you might get a girl pregnant.

Well, certainly all three problems can be consequences of sexual activity outside of marriage, but notice something very important. In all of those reasons for abstaining, God is nowhere to be found! Those arguments support the same case for purity that anyone in the world could make. So I guess it shouldn't surprise us that young people growing up in Christian homes hearing these motives for living lives of character aren't keeping themselves any purer than the children of the world. It shouldn't surprise us, but it should teach us a lesson. Christians have a totally different reason for practicing purity than people in the world. The only motive we need is that we are subjects of a King who expects purity, and we need to be living as subjects of the

King. And, if we expect our people to live lives of character, we'd better start giving them reasons based on allegiance to a God of character.

Character begins with God! A life of character must be built on the right foundation, for true character is the result of our beliefs. What I mean is, we're unlikely to tell the truth when doing so will put us in a jam, unless we care more about God's valuing honesty than we care about our own comfort. And, when the waitress makes an error in our favor on the ticket, we probably won't point it out, unless we are more concerned with God's desire that we deal honestly with others than we are about saving a few cents.

God, not man, is the changeless center by which right and wrong are determined.

People of character realize that the only motivation sufficient to keep us living a life of character is a complete love for and allegiance to a God who values character. They acknowledge that God, not man, is the changeless center by which right and wrong are determined.

No Place but First Place

Did you notice that the first instruction does not start, "You shall believe in a god"? That is not necessary. We've spent a number of centuries trying to hide this fact, but man has a built-in need for God. Foxholes and hospital rooms have been revealing that need for centuries. In fact, not only does every person have a need for God, but every person has a god, as well. That statement may surprise you, but it's true. A god is whatever has first place in your life. In every person's heart, there is a throne; and on every throne, there is a god. The only question, then, is whether that god is true or false.

The God of the Bible declares that he will not accept any place in your life but first place: *You shall have no other gods before me* (Exodus 20:3). The first instruction asserts God's claim to be our only legitimate foundation. In fact, without this fundamental declaration of his sovereign right to be the only one on our heart's throne, all the rest of the instructions make no difference. Until we commit to the first principle, it doesn't matter to us what God says about stealing or adultery, because we haven't yet acknowledged his right to legislate those areas of our lives. We, not he, are still the moral center. And the great lie of the Garden is perpetuated.

So we start with the only place we can start in building a life of character—asking the question, "Who is going to sit on the throne in my heart? Who will be the foundation on which I will build my life?" God says, "Put me first."

The "Gods" Who Would Be King

Just as all character is a result of putting the true God on the throne of our hearts, all sins are a result of putting other gods on that throne. Jehovah has as much competition for our hearts today as ever before. Too often we make the mistake of thinking that Satan is antireligion. He's not. He doesn't even mind our worshiping Jehovah, as long as we mix in a few other gods for good measure. In fact, Satan doesn't mind our choosing good or even doing good sometimes—as long as we're doing it because *we* think it's a good idea. What Satan objects to is our doing good because we have put God first. Yes, Satan is crafty—so crafty that he can even entice those of us desiring to be people of character to follow the siren calls of other "gods."

Oh, we don't worship Mars (the god of war) today. But how much do we put our trust and our security in making certain that the United States' military complex can outgun any other country in the world? And I have driven around Fort Worth, Texas, for a few years now, and I have yet to see a single temple where people can worship the sex goddess Aphrodite. But I can assure you, a great many people here do worship sex. And they do in your home town, too.

> *This first principle is the keystone of God's entire plan for developing his character in his people.*

A "god" is anything in which we put our trust and focus. That can be a job, a relationship, a political system, money, even ourselves—anything we look to as our ultimate source of strength. Whether or not we call the object of our trust a "god" is not the point. The point is that people of character put their trust in Jehovah God and him alone. Relying on anything else usurps his throne and undermines his authority as King. Visualize a stone archway. The wedge-shaped piece of rock at the crown of the arch is the keystone. It locks the other pieces in place. All of the other rocks depend on the keystone for support. It's easy to see that this first principle is the keystone of God's entire plan for developing his character in his people. All the other principles depend on this keystone.

One way to interpret or elaborate on the remaining points in God's Code of Ethics is to see them as applications of the first principle. We are not to have any other gods before the LORD God. Therefore, when the fourth principle says to set aside one day a week to rest and reflect and honor God, the idea behind it is, "Don't let work be your god. Don't try to build your life on the foundation of your career." God knows that such an existence will not survive life's storms.

In the sixth instruction, God says, "Do not kill." How many of us have been hurt or violated by someone? Perhaps you were the victim of abuse from people you loved and trusted. Is that pain consuming you? Is that dominating you so that you can't seem to think about anything else? In other words, the sixth instruction says, "Don't let your hatred be your god." You can't build a life of character when hatred is on the throne in your heart.

> *You can't build a life of character when hatred is on the throne in your heart.*

God also says, "Don't commit adultery." God is not against sex. He created sex and made us sexual beings. But he's given us an avenue, a channel through which to express and fulfill our sexual drives. Some of us, however, think we need more sex, in different places, with more partners, etc. Too often, we fall into the trap of thinking this slavery to the "sex god" (which has been billed by Satan as "sexual freedom") is the key to living life to the fullest. But God says we're heading for a fatal crash anytime we let sex become our god. We can't build lives of character on a foundation like that.

We now come to the eighth instruction, "Don't steal" and the tenth, "Don't covet." Do you know what they are saying? "Don't let "things" be your god." I don't know about you, but I need to hear that. Right now, I live in the nicest house I have ever lived in, and I drive the nicest car I have ever owned, yet I still catch myself saying to myself, "If I could just live on that street . . ." or "If I could just drive one of those, I'd be happier." But God says, "No!" You can't build a life that lasts on things that don't.

God's instruction to the Israelites to have "no other gods before me" was truly revolutionary in that time (and still is today), for God is not saying other gods should rank behind him in importance. He is not calling for the Israelites to worship him as the dominant god, but as the only one. In fact, God said in Exodus 34:14, "Do not worship any other god, for the LORD, whose name is Jealous, is a jealous God."

God says "No!" You can't build a life that lasts on things that don't.

It used to confuse me that God would say he was jealous, because we've given that word a negative connotation. But now as a husband, I understand that sometimes jealousy is not a flaw, but a moral excellence. I have a holy jealousy toward my wife Jamie. We have made a covenant with each other— we made a solemn agreement before God—to share our lives and love with each other, and I'm jealous of that covenant because it is destroyed if we share it with any other. I want her sole affection, or the covenant is broken.

Have you ever been on a tour of a castle? When the guide takes you to the throne room and points out the throne, there is one thing I can guarantee: it will be a seat for one. There's just no such thing as a throne "pew." Thrones come in all sizes, shapes, and styles, but the one thing they all have in common is that they are made for a lone occupant. And the first step toward building a life of character is deciding that Jehovah God will be the lone occupant on the throne of your own heart.

The God Who Should Be King

When God began addressing the children of Israel at Mount Sinai, God began with a revelation about himself, for his plan for building character in us can only be understood in relation to the character of God. Beginning to know Jehovah is crucial to our quest for character, for he is the definition of character. So, before he tells us what he wants, God tells us who he is.

The Unchanging God

He begins by saying, "I am the LORD" (Exodus 20:2). That word, "LORD," might be in all capitals in your Bible. Some versions of the Bible might say "Jehovah" or "Yahweh." We don't know exactly how to pronounce that personal name of God. We find it in Exodus 3 when Moses stood before a burning bush. There, God instructed him to return to Egypt and deliver God's people. When Moses said to God that the people would want to know the name of the one who had sent him, God told Moses to tell the people that God's name—his personal covenant name—is "I AM." That's what the word literally means. Another way of translating the word is "I AM WHO I AM," or "I Will Be that I Will Be." This strange name is indicative of God's unchanging character. His own name means that God is absolutely faithful to his word and to himself. Therefore, when God introduces these principles by telling us who he is, he is saying, "I deserve first place in your life simply because I am the I AM." He always is, and he always is the same. That's why we can talk about the permanent relevance of God's values.

To grasp the moral absoluteness of the Ten Commandments, we have to grasp the eternal nature of the unchangeable One who authored them. If God were changeable, then his values might be changeable as well. That's why human laws are always changing. Some years ago, for example, the U.S. Supreme Court wrote the legal definition of "obscenity." The court basically said that something is obscene if it is considered so by the local community. The court wrote this definition hoping it would stand the test of time, but do you know what is wrong with this definition? It makes the definition contingent on the values of changeable people. Thus, we are being exposed to literature, movies, and artwork today that ten years ago would have been considered obscene, but which our "communities" no longer find shocking. What has changed—the content of the material, or the people who are the materials' judges?

I AM is still I AM.
He will never be He Was.

In the same way, someone may say, "I know God said a long time ago not to commit adultery, but these are different times." Yes, times have changed, but God has not. He is who he is. He's always been who he is, and he's always going to be who he is. Stealing will always be wrong. Lying will always be wrong. Harming your neighbor will always be wrong because I AM is still I AM. He will never be He Was. Jehovah's character is something we can count on. He is the unchangeable reference point, the constant moral center, the pivot point for all decisions we must make. So we start right here: "I am the LORD your God."

The Personal God

An interesting thing to note about that word *your* in the phrase "your God" is that it is actually singular rather than plural. In other words, instead of saying "I'm the national God of Israel," God is saying "I'm the personal God of each Israelite. I'm the God of Abraham, the God of Moses, the God of Aaron, the God of Joshua, the God of Miriam."

"Your God" implies that this eternal I AM knows you and me, and even more incredibly perhaps, wants to be known by you and me. He wants a relationship with us so much, in fact that, rather than waiting for us to initiate it, he takes the first step. God always approaches us before we approach him. The importance of this point is that as his eternal nature gives him the right to rule, his love and proximity give me the desire to follow.

Let me illustrate. George Washington is the father of my country. I respect George Washington, and I'm grateful for what he did for the United States. I do not, however, love George Washington, nor do I feel compelled by his contributions to this country to pattern my life after his. On the other hand, James Morgan Atchley is my father. He raised me, invested his life in me, and was available to me when I needed him. The respect and love I feel toward James Morgan Atchley and my obedience to him while I lived in his home are the results of his personal interest in and commitment to me. He is my personal father. So it is with Jehovah. His love is as constant as his eternal holiness. I am moved to *want* to obey this great God who cares enough about me to want to be my personal God.

The Delivering God

Just as God wants to be God of each person, he also wants to be God of a people, and he reminds the Israelites that he is the God who "brought you out of Egypt." Only three months before, they had been a people of bondage in Egypt. There they had been exposed to many "gods." Now they were on the threshold of a new land—Canaan—where they would be enticed by as many imposter gods as ever. And God is calling the Israelites to take a stand; he's saying it is time for them to commit their allegiance to him. After all, he is the one who delivered them from those imposter Egyptian gods. He tells the Israelites in the first instruction, "I want your allegiance because of who I am. (*I am the eternal God.*) I want your allegiance because of where I am. (*I am close to you.*) And I want your allegiance because of what I do. (*I am your deliverer.*)

He hasn't changed. He is still the LORD God, the living I AM. He is still the personal God who invests himself in our lives. And he is still the God who delivers—who, as Paul wrote to the Colossians, "rescued us from the dominion of darkness and brought us into the kingdom of the Son he loves, in whom we have redemption, the forgiveness of sins" (Colossians 1:13). Just as he delivered the Israelites out of bondage to the Egyptians, he is still delivering his children today out of bondage to Satan.

We can trust a God like that. In fact, if we try to make anyone or anything else our foundation, we're building our lives on something that cannot withstand the tests of time and trouble. Other "gods" simply can't deliver. They are illegitimate contenders for the thrones of our hearts. Only Jehovah God belongs there.

A Test to See Who Is King

I suppose the twenty-thousand-dollar-question, then, is, "How do I put God on that throne?" Here's my advice: *begin by identifying what's in second place.* It's just human nature for us to want to give the "right" answer instead of the truthful one when asked what's in first place in our hearts. Too often, we're like the junior high school girl on a church retreat. The camp director was trying to get a discussion going. So, thinking he'd start with a really easy question, he asked the kids, "What's furry and gray, has a big fluffy tail, and eats nuts?" To his amazement the kids seemed to be in a quandary over his question. Finally, one little girl raised her hand rather tentatively and answered, "It sounds like a squirrel, but I'll say Jesus Christ." Sometimes with "religious" questions, it's just hard to "tell it like it is."

So make it easy on yourself. Find out what's in second place in your heart, and closely monitor whatever that is. For most of us, it will probably be a good thing—a career, a family, maybe even a ministry. I must confess that one of the things I have to constantly monitor is my love for preaching. Early in my ministry, I realized that I would have to guard my heart to make sure my love of preaching would never overtake my love for God. Does that seem strange to you? Nevertheless, I have to consciously put God first, so that if God ever wants me to go somewhere or do something that requires leaving the pulpit, I'll be willing to go. It's hard for ministers to realize that good things can sometimes become "other gods." It's hard for other people to realize that, too. A word to the wise: Watch what's in second place. Like baseball legend Satchel Paige said, "Something may be gaining on you."

After you've identified God's "competition," make conscious decisions to put him first. Again, though, the hard question is "How do I do that?" Try using this acronym to give you a place to start: F-I-R-S-T. Here are five areas in your life to check to see if, when the hard decisions come, you are putting God first.

Focus. What is your focus? Most of the nonbelievers I know are not people who deny the existence of God, but are people who over time have simply lost sight of him. It's amazing how easy it is to go through the routine of life, even going to church, and still rarely think about God.

Perhaps you've heard the story about the lady who was leaving church one Sunday and saw a friend. She asked her friend, "Did you notice that hat Myrtle was wearing?"

"No, I didn't notice," her friend replied.

"Well," the first woman tried again, "what about the coat that Hazel had on?"

"Sorry, I didn't notice that, either," the friend replied once again.

"Well," the first woman harrumphed, "a lot of good it does *you* to go to church!" Even at church some people lose their focus.

But I'm not just talking about our focus while we're at church. What do you think about in free-thought time? When you're taking a shower, mowing the yard, riding your bike, out for a jog, commuting to work? Every day you've got some time just to think. What do you think about? Whatever it is that occupies your thoughts, it is probably something very close to your heart. Do you think about God?

Moses told the Israelites to fill their lives reflecting on and sharing God's plan for his people of character. He said, "Impress [the commandments] on your children. Talk about them when you sit at home and when you walk along the road, when you lie down and when you get up" (Deuteronomy 6:7). The reason that this loving God gives is "that you may enjoy long life" (verse 2b) and "that it may go well with you" (verse 3b).

Impress [the commandments] on your children.

The focus of our thoughts is important because it's an indicator of the purpose of our lives. We should focus on the bull's eye. Is God in the middle of your target? He was in the middle of Christ's. Do you remember when the disciples went to get Jesus some food in John 4:34? They brought it back and said in essence, "Here's your lunch, Lord." And Jesus replied, "My food is to do the will of him who sent me and to finish his work." Do you find yourself thinking about God like that?

Jesus of Nazareth was the only man to live a really full life, a life of true moral character, on this earth. Interestingly, he was also the only man to fully, completely, and constantly keep the first principle. He never let anyone or anything compete with his allegiance to the LORD God. And he never said, "I'm empty." He never wondered if he were building his life on the wrong foundation.

Income. A modern biographer's research isn't complete until he reviews his subject's check stubs. In fact, there might be no better indicator in modern America of what a person values than what he does with his money. Of course, this thought isn't new. It's exactly what Jesus was telling us in Matthew 6:21, 24b when he said, "For where your treasure is, there your heart will be also. You cannot serve both God and Money." I like the way the Living Bible translates Deuteronomy 14:23, when it says "The purpose of tithing is to teach you always to put God first in your lives."

Relationships. Our relationships with other people tell us much about our love for God. John says, "If anyone says, 'I love God,' yet hates his brother, he is a liar. For anyone who does not love his brother, whom he has seen, cannot love God, whom he has not seen" (1 John 4:20). All the parts of God's plan are interrelated. Any time we violate our neighbor by stealing, any time we violate our neighbor by lying, any time we hurt our neighbor through injury, murder, or adultery, we've broken the first commandment. If we are putting God first, all our relationships will fall into one of two categories: (1) the people we choose to be around because they bring us closer to God; or, (2) the people we choose to be around because we can bring them closer to God.

Security. The last time you needed some support, the last time you needed something or someone to lean on, where did you turn first? It seems to me we often turn to God last. Too often, we're like the man lying in the hospital bed as the doctor comes in to give him the test results. "I'm afraid all we can do now is pray," the doctor said. "Oh dear," responded the patient, "has it come to that?"

Remember that in Matthew 6, Jesus said that whether or not we worry is a sign of whether or not we are putting God first. How much do you worry? If you're worried about many things, you're having trouble with the throne room in your heart. Jesus' advice in verse 33 is, "Seek first his kingdom and his righteousness." Then, when we've put our focus where it belongs, Jesus says God will take care of all the things we worry about. Peter repeats this same idea later when he says, "Cast all your anxiety on him because he cares for you" (1 Peter 5:7).

Time. Besides wanting to see our check stubs, a biographer in modern America would also want to see our Daytimers®. How a person makes appointments reveals a lot about that person. What do we schedule in; what do we schedule out? I'm not talking just about showing up for church on Sundays (although that's included). One day a week is not what God wants. Suppose I said to Jamie one night, "Honey, I want you to know that I am going to be absolutely, totally faithful to you one day every week. No, I mean it; that day is yours. I promise." Do you think she would be pleased with that arrangement? I feel pretty safe in saying she would not.

But if I'm going to give more than that to my relationship with God, I have to do it on purpose, so I make appointments with God. I schedule time that I'm going to keep totally reserved for him just like I schedule all the events I plan that are important to me. Jesus did the same thing. Oh, I don't mean he had a Daytimer®, but he did purposely plan and spend time with his Father. In Mark 1:35, we read that "very early in the morning, while it was still dark, Jesus got up, left the house and went off to a solitary place, where he prayed." Why did Jesus do that? Because he was obeying the first principle. It's a principle that's got to be reaffirmed every day. We must wake up every morning praying, "God, help me put you first today." We must go to bed at night and reflect, "Was Jesus my Lord today?" The Today's English Version states Colossians 1:18b like this: "[Christ] was raised from death, in order that he alone might have the first place in all things."

A Higher Compass

Before the days of modern navigational aids, ships crossing the Atlantic Ocean used two separate compasses. One was fixed to the deck where the steerman could see it and try to keep the ship on course. The other compass was fastened at the top of one of the masts, and often a sailor would climb up to check it to be certain they were still on course.

On one such voyage a passenger asked the ship's captain, "Why do you have two compasses?"

The captain replied, "This is an iron vessel, and the compass on the deck is often affected by its surroundings. That's not the case with the compass at the masthead; that one is above the influence of what's around us. We steer by the compass above because it's more reliable. It's safer."

And that's why we should steer our lives under the direction of God above. As human beings we are often affected by our surroundings. God is beyond the influence of what's around us. He alone is the unchangeable, sure, and reliable moral center by which right and wrong are determined. Steering our lives by his Code of Ethics is the only way to travel in a quest. It's safer. We must learn to put God first.

Focusing Your Faith

1. God put *you* first by dying on the cross because of your sins. What does the New Testament teach about a "cross-centered ethic"? (See 1 Corinthians 6 and Ephesians 4 for two examples.)

2. Imagine that you are an account executive with a marketing firm that has been hired to mount an ad campaign to improve America's character. What is the first ad we would see?

3. If you turned on your radio, and God's theme song was playing, what song do you think you would hear?

4. What are some ways Jesus modeled obedience to the first principles?

5. "Every person has a need for God. And every person has a god as well. Identify the "gods" you've put on a throne.

6. What are some of the good things you must monitor so that they stay in second place?

7. Name some specific ways you can improve your relationship to God by putting him first over something or someone in your life.

Chapter 4

Right God, Wrong Image

∽

There is a temple in Kyoto, Japan, called The Temple of the Thousand Buddhas. Inside this temple are 1,000 statues of Buddha, each one slightly different than any of the others in the

> **Principle 2:**
>
> *Take God as He Is*
>
> *Exodus 20:4-6*
> *2 Corinthians 3:17, 18*

temple so that the worshiper can go in, find the image of Buddha that looks most like himself, and worship that one.

Indeed, this tendency to shape God into our own image has been so prevalent throughout human history that Emil Durkheim, a famous sociologist, devised his Theory of Reification, which said basically that religion is a fraud—a guise under which selfish human beings justify and rationalize their pursuits by giving them divine endorsements. In other words, if one group of people wants to go to war and conquer the people around them, they create war gods, because war gods promote war. If the people want to have sex with whomever they please, they conjure up love gods, because love gods endorse free love. The eighteenth-century philosopher, Montesquieu, offered the same sentiment when he wrote, "If triangles had a god, he would have three sides."

What we really seem to want are user-friendly gods. We want a god who is like us. We want to reshape God to fit our own needs. Satan doesn't mind our worshiping Jehovah God—as long as we reshape God into a form that suits our (really Satan's) purpose.

---

*We want to reshape God to fit
our own needs.*

Many might wonder why it is so important to deal with our relationship to God if it is our character defects that need the most attention. "After all," they would argue, "this is just theology, isn't it? It's not real life." Of course, we know better. In God's plan, there's no such thing as a theology that consists merely of intellectual beliefs. All that God reveals to us about himself and his plan for us is meant to impact and improve our minds *and* our actions.

Victory at this early stage of character development is important to Satan for the same reason that it is important to God. The decision of whom to worship controls the direction of our lives. For Satan, getting us to commit external sins is merely winning a spiritual skirmish, but getting us to choose another god or to serve a perverted image of

God is to win the decisive battle of the war for our souls! After that victory is accomplished, all sorts of moral defeats are ensured.

So, before God ever begins to discuss the kind of behavior he wants his people of character to exhibit, he talks about the direction their lives need to take. His plan says first, "Put me first," and second, "Accept me for who I am." In Exodus 20:4, God instructs Israel,

> *You shall not make for yourself an idol in the form of anything in heaven above or on the earth beneath or in the waters below. You shall not bow down to them or worship them; for I, the LORD your God, am a jealous God, punishing the children for the sin of the fathers to the third and fourth generation of those who hate me, but showing love to a thousand generations of those who love me and keep my commandments.*

Our Attempts at Shaping God

Centuries ago, the Latin church father Augustine defined *idolatry* as "worshiping anything that ought to be used or using anything that ought to be worshiped." And it is this second type of idolatry that God is discussing in the second principle of his Code of Ethics. In the first principle God has already warned of the dangers of worshiping idols representing false gods, but in the second principle he is forbidding false worship of the true God. God is warning us of the dangers of our making representations of himself.

Too often, we underrate the significance of what God is trying to tell us here about living lives of character. In fact, many of us don't see how the

second principle relates to modern life at all. We're
like the two men walking into church services one
morning who looked up at the marquee and read,
"This week's sermon: The Ten Commandments." One
man looked at the other and said, "Well, at least I
haven't made any graven images lately." The fact is,
though, we don't have to employ goldsmiths or
woodcutters to try our hand at shaping God. The
practice of trying to shape a "*user*-friendly" god is all
too common.

As illogical as it may seem in view of the mess
we're all in, most people have decided that it is
preferable to try to shape God into their own image
rather than to change their image to match his.

---

*Before we ever have metal images of
God, we have mental ones.*

Of course, we are speaking of pagans, aren't we?
Christians would never dare to use our God this
way—or would we? We may not be so blatant about
what we're doing as pagan people are, but Christians fall into this trap as well. As the French writer,
Voltaire, described the situation, "If God created us
in his own image, we have more than reciprocated."

Before we ever have metal images of God, we have
mental ones. Even if we haven't translated our
mental image into silver or gold, it's idolatry none-
theless. We are like the four-year-old boy whose
Sunday school teacher asked what he was drawing.
"I'm drawing a picture of God," replied the little boy.
Amused, the teacher probed further, "How can you
do that, since no one knows what God looks like?"
The boy kept right on drawing, and, without missing
a beat, replied, "They will when I'm through."

What are some of the images of God we might
have that dishonor him? The list is probably endless,
but here are a few I've come across in my years of
ministry:
• One popular image here in America is that of God
as Uncle Sam. His motto is "America, love it or leave
it." Is that your God? He's the God that endorses
anything the United States wants to do, buy, sell, or
fight. He's the God that says, "If you're a good Christian, you're a good American." If you worship this
God, your values and actions will be more heavily
influenced by your concept of national security and
reputation than by purity or justice.
• Or how about God as George Burns? His motto is
"Let's be buddies." He wears a fishing cap, boots, and
a coat. He's your pal; he's your friend. He's the guy
across the street. If he is your God, all he wants from
you is for you to be a good ol' boy, and he'll be happy
to help you through the rough times. Sure, you've
got a few bad habits. Who hasn't? Just be better
than most of the people around you, and you'll be
okay.
• Very popular during the eighties, the God as
Donald Trump model is still in vogue with some—
especially the televangelists. The Donald deity says,
"You *can* have it all. God wants you to have everything. Just send some money, and it will come back
to you 20-, 50-, or 100-fold." This God never wants
Christians to be sick, sad, or suffer in any way. And
if you're experiencing one of these nasty "S" words, it
must be your lack of faith (or contributions). If you
worship this God, you don't have to give a moment's
thought to the poor, the hungry, or the suffering,
because they wouldn't be poor, hungry, or suffering
unless they deserved it. And what's more, you can
get as wrapped up in material things as you want,
because God wouldn't have given them to you if you

didn't deserve them.

• Another widespread image of God is that of a Big Vending Machine in the Sky. We put our quarter in (by saying our prayers, doing our good deeds, or in some other way putting God in our debt), and then we wait for God to send us our candy bar. After all, we paid for it didn't we? If you worship this God, you believe that if you do enough good deeds, you can put God in your debt. He will owe you good things (especially in the life to come). And, best of all, it doesn't matter at all what kind of attitude you have while you do your good deeds. You can hate whomever you please, resent others' taking advantage of you, feel superior to anyone not doing as much as you are (because God doesn't owe them as much) and it won't matter at all to God. As long as you keep inserting those quarters, he *has* to give you something in return.

Whom you worship determines who you are.

• There are many other images of God, of course. There's God as Santa Claus. His motto is "Now what can I bring you next?" If you worship him, you are justified in doing *anything* that you think will make you happy.

• Or how about God as Monte Hall? His motto is "Let's make a deal." If you worship him, you can do whatever you like until you get in a jam, then he'll negotiate how much good behavior it will take to get you out of trouble.

The images go on and on and on. And the point is this: When we shape God into a more "suitable" image, we can then excuse unsuitable character qualities. There is no doubt that whom you worship determines who you are.

Even as Jesus walked the face of the earth, he encountered people trying to reshape what he was trying to do and be. For example, when Jesus told the disciples that, rather than reigning on earth as a glorious king of Israel, the Messiah would die on a cross, Peter rebuked him (Mark 8:31-33). This scenario certainly did not fit Peter's scheme of things. Peter was looking for a God who would give him military and political power. It was clear (to Peter, at least) that God needed to change. At this point, Peter was the fiery disciple willing to kill to advance the Messiah's earthly kingdom—one in which he expected a position of power. It wasn't until he accepted Jesus as the crucified Savior that Peter could call himself "a servant" (2 Peter 1:1).

So why do we try to reshape God? Because shaping him into our image is easier than being shaped into his. It fits our purposes to reshape God, for a divine power who endorses everything that we already want can come in very handy.

What's Wrong with Idolatry?

We don't want an "off-the-rack" deity. We want a custom-tailored God—one who will stand for the things we think are important, condemn the things that don't cramp our style, and wink at our little idiosyncrasies. My wife worked with a woman once, for example, who left her husband and moved in with another man, even though the woman insisted she still believed in God. When Jamie tried to talk to the woman about the inconsistency between the way she was living and being an obedient disciple, the woman's reply was, "I just believe God wants me to be happy." She worshiped the Santa Claus God. You

see, the God of the Bible didn't fit her lifestyle. She
was really saying, "Let it out a little in the seventh
commandment. This is a little too tight for me."

What do you want to do? What do you want to be?
What do you want to have? Then shape God so that
he thinks it's okay. That is idolatry. It is using the
one who ought to be worshiped. And it's what we've
been doing now for century after century—changing
God so that *we* don't have to change.

In the final analysis, idolatry is really just a subtle
form of self-worship. It humanizes God while it
deifies man. And God says idolatry is something we
cannot play around with if we are to build lives of
character. Why? Because God cannot be imaged.

---

*Anytime we try to shape God, we
de-emphasize some facets of his character because we emphasize others.*

If you think about it, most distorted images of God
contain some grain of truth, but they are the result
of focusing so much on one particular facet of his
character that other qualities important to God are
left out of the picture.

Do you like bad pictures of yourself? Why do
people hate to show others their driver's license?
Mine looks like it belongs on a "wanted" poster in
the post office. Don't you think that the God who
made heaven and earth is extremely offended when
we make these pitiful, ludicrous pictures of him and
call them "his likeness"?

Anytime we try to shape God, we de-emphasize
some facets of his character because we emphasize
others. That was one of the problems with Aaron's
golden bull. Exodus 32 gives us the account of the

Israelites' first departure from God's plan for
character. Moses was up on the mountain talking
with God. Moses had been gone for some time, and
the children of Israel were getting anxious, so they
approached Aaron, the high priest, for instructions.
Aaron told the people to bring their gold to him, and
when they did, he used the gold to shape a calf or a
bull. "Tomorrow," Aaron tells the people, "there will
be a festival to the LORD" (Exodus 32:5) . . . before
God, the I AM, Yahweh.

Now, Aaron had the right God, but he had the
wrong image. He wasn't trying to bring in a new god.
Instead, he was trying to comfort the people by
providing some tangible likeness to represent that
formless power who was meeting with their leader.
Aaron chose the bull as the figure to represent
Yahweh because, to the ancients, the bull was a
symbol of power. Clearly, Yahweh was a God of
power, for he destroyed the Egyptians and freed the
Israelites. But to say only that God is powerful does
not give an adequate description of the LORD.

*Anytime we try to reshape our perfect
God, all we do is distort him.*

What about his holiness? The figure of a bull says
nothing about God's righteousness, which explains
how the children of Israel could be worshiping the
LORD and having an orgy all at the same time. Anytime we try to reshape our perfect God, all we do is
distort him. And if we worship a distorted God, we
will be a distorted people.

When Moses spoke to the people just before he
died, he reminded them of the day they heard the
Code of Ethics from the mountain. He said in

Deuteronomy 4:12, "Then the LORD spoke to you out
of the fire. You heard the sound of words but saw no
form; there was only a voice." God reveals himself to
us as he pleases, and we have neither the right nor
the understanding to represent him adequately
outside of what he has revealed.

God Will Not Stay Put

Another reason we "image" God is so he will "stay
put." But God can't be confined. Do you remember a
movie that came out years ago called *Cool Hand
Luke*? Luke, played by Paul Newman, is driving
down the road in his car while a figure of Christ
dangles from the rearview mirror. As he speeds
recklessly down the road, Luke sings at the top of
his lungs, "I don't care if it rains or freezes, as long
as I've got my plastic Jesus." It's nice to know where
God is, just in case we need him, isn't it?

Unfortunately, characters in movies aren't the
only ones who would like to pinpoint God's location
for their own benefit. There was once a lady who, in
effect, asked Jesus, "Listen, you Jews say that God
lives down in Jerusalem in the temple, but my
fathers say he lives up here on this mountain. So I'm
confused about where to go to find God when it's
time to go to church. Where does God stay put?" And
Jesus replied, basically, "God doesn't stay put." As
John 4:24 records Jesus' words: "God is spirit, and
his worshipers must worship in spirit and in truth."

How does it affect our character when we try to
keep God "in his place"? The main impact on us is
that if God is assigned to one location—the temple,
or a church building, perhaps—then the only thing
we have to worry about is keeping our appointment
with him there. We can do what we want when we're
not in his presence, because he'll either be ignorant

or indifferent to it. If we could just make God "stay put," he wouldn't be concerned with morals, but only with ritual. Regular church attendance would be more important than right character. Perhaps that explains why the woman inquiring of God's where-abouts had been married five times and was cur-rently living with a man who was not her husband. She thought God was in some specific physical location—obviously *not* in her own home and life.

Jesus spent a great deal of energy trying to ex-plain this concept during his earthly ministry. And some of the most religious people of his day were the ones who had the hardest time understanding his point. The group of Jews known as the Pharisees believed that ritual and external adherence to God's commands were all that God asked of people. But Jesus gave his assessment of their character:

> "Woe to you, teachers of the law and Pharisees, you hypocrites! You give a tenth of your spices— mint, dill and cummin. But you have neglected the more important matters of the law—justice, mercy and faithfulness. You should have prac-ticed the latter, without neglecting the former. . . . You clean the outside of the cup and dish, but inside they are full of greed and self-indulgence. Blind Pharisee! First clean the inside of the cup and dish, and then the outside also will be clean" (Matthew 23:23- 26).

Jesus knew that our character comes from the inside out. And our character must be based on a God that is aware of both our actions *and* our atti-tudes wherever we are.

Another interesting aspect of our trying to pin God down to a certain place is that we tend to picture him as being "up there" orbiting the earth like the

starship *Enterprise* in *Star Trek*. We think he stays
directly over whatever spot we or our interests
happen to inhabit at the moment. That means, of
course, that his eyes are always focused on us and
our concerns. *You* (in other words, anyone else in the
world who doesn't have exactly my points of view
and/or interests) have to do something to divert
God's attention from *me* and *my* concerns if *you* need
something. It's hard for us to grasp the concept of a
God who is just as aware of a Kurd or Serb or Croat
or Masai as he is of you and me, but that's the God of
the Bible. He is *all*-knowing and all present.

> ### You can't build a box for God and
> ### tell him to stay there.

One night when our son Michael was four, as
Jamie was putting him to bed he looked up at her
and asked, "Mom, how can God be here *and* in San
Antonio (where his grandparents and cousins live) at
the same time?" Jamie tried to explain that because
God is a spirit, he doesn't have a body like ours that
can only be in one place at a time, and he can truly
be everywhere in the world all at once. Michael lay
there for a moment trying to absorb this and, finally,
looked up with a puzzled expression and said, "You
mean he's smeared?" I'm not sure the concept is
much clearer to many of us than it was to Michael
that night.

Try as we might to chain God to our interests, he
won't stay put. You can't build a box for God and tell
him to stay there. Solomon knew all about trying to
house God. After he had spent all that time and all
that money building a magnificent, glorious temple
for the LORD, Solomon and the people waited for God

to "move in." As God filled the temple with his
Spirit, Solomon prayed, "The heavens, even the
highest heaven, cannot contain you. How much less
this temple I've built" (1 Kings 8:27).

A minister walked into church one day and neglected to take off his hat. An elderly lady from the
congregation saw the man walking around with his
hat on and indignantly approached him, berating
him, saying, "How dare you wear that hat in the
church?" Without missing a beat, the minister
replied, "Ma'am, this hat is *on* the church!" That
lady, probably with the best of intentions, had
decided she knew where God lived. It was okay to do
some things outside of his presence (in this case,
wearing hats) that were unacceptable in his presence. And even though we may be amused at her
concern, we need to remind ourselves of the pitfalls
of her mistake. People of character walk around with
God *in* them (1 Corinthians 6:19, 20). We live as
people in the presence of our King.

God Will Not Be Used

Another reason God refuses to be imaged is that
he refuses to be manipulated. The Israelites had a
hard time learning this lesson. God gave the Israelites the ark of the covenant as a symbol of all that he
had done for them. They, however, consistently
viewed the ark as a religious talisman that they
could use against their foes. First Samuel 4 provides
an account of a battle in which the Israelites were
defeated by the Philistines. After the defeat, the
Israelites concluded that the only sure-fire way to
win the battle the next day was to bring the ark into
the midst of the fight. They said, "Let us bring the
ark of the LORD's covenant from Shiloh, so that it
may go with us and save us from the hand of our

enemies" (verse 3). God was so displeased with the
Israelites for using the ark to attempt to force him
into stamping approval on their battle that he gave
the Philistines an even greater victory that day than
the day before. And, he allowed them to capture the
ark. As the Israelites discovered that day, we can't
manipulate God for our own purposes. He's not our
own religious version of "lightning in a bottle."

Perhaps this frustration with God's elusive nature
also helps explain our tendency to look for formulas,
plans, or 1-2-3 steps that give us the inside track on
how to control God. Yes, our idols—our more comfortable, tangible representations of God—are certainly easier to live with than the Almighty God of
all creation, for the Almighty has an unsettling habit
of always surprising us just when we think we have
him figured out.

For many of us, it is hard to accept that God
reveals himself to us when he wants and as he
wants. It is much more comfortable to believe we
have him "pegged." We want to shape him into
something our minds can handle so that we can
know exactly who he is and where he is, and we can
accurately predict in any given situation what he
will do. We can surely use that knowledge to our
own advantage. But God is too big for that kind of
manipulation. We were designed to meet his purposes, not the other way around.

What's wrong with shaping God into a convenient
image? It's asking God to be the instrument through
which we worship and deify ourselves. Idolatry
inevitably leads to an erosion of reverence. We don't
strive to reach God anymore. Instead, we bring God
down to our level. God knows that if we are to live
lives of character, we need to remember our place in
the scheme of things. He is the Master Potter that
created us out of the clay. God's greatest honor to us

was that he made us in his image. And our greatest
dishonor to God is to try to remake him in ours.

God's Plan for Shaping Us

In some ways, I wish I could have been there at
Sinai when the voice of God delivered his Code of
Ethics, his principles for living, but I would never
trade places with anyone in the encampment that
day. God at Sinai gave us a word, a voice. God at
Bethlehem gave us a face; he gave us Immanuel,
"God with us." We have God's self-portrait. What
other image do we need?

To Reveal Himself to Us

It's very tempting to want a single snapshot of
God, to find one facet of his character and build our
worship around that aspect of God. But what he
asks is for us to read his book and look at the entire
photo album. If we'll look at the whole album—the
Bible—his Word will start to convict us of his love,
his holiness, his justice, his grace, his wrath, his
righteousness, his faithfulness. And the list goes on
and on. Then, after we've read his Book cover to
cover, we'll know in truth that he is too huge to
be represented . . . too unfathomable to be understood . . . too mysterious to be predicted. As Isaiah
said, "Who has understood the mind of the LORD, or
instructed him as his counselor?" (Isaiah 40:13). Yet
even the mystery surrounding God helps build
character because it reminds us that we are the ones
made of dust, not him. It reminds us of God's maj-
esty and unmatched glory. And we must stay
humble before him.

How can we, who cannot begin to grasp a God so
big, presume to make an image of him? There has
only been one tangible image of God that has

captured him—only one that does not reduce him. But that image was made by God, not man, and announced by angels: Jesus Christ, God in the flesh. Paul refers to Christ as "the image of God" (2 Corinthians 4:4), and as "the image of the invisible God" (Colossians 1:15). The writer of Hebrews said, "The Son is the radiance of God's glory and the exact representation of his being" (1:3). And, of course, no one said it plainer than did Jesus as he comforted his disciples just before his death, "Anyone who has seen me has seen the Father" (John 14:9).

To Reshape Us into Himself

It comes down to this, then: God is not the one with the image problem. We are. We are the ones whose image has been scarred and marred by sin. But I've got good news for you! If we'll take God as he is, he will take us as we are. And what's even better, he won't leave us where he found us! Instead, he'll begin to reshape us into the image he always intended us to have—his own. As Paul writes:

> Now the Lord is the Spirit, and where the Spirit of the Lord is, there is freedom. And we, who with unveiled faces all reflect the Lord's glory, are being transformed into his likeness with ever-increasing glory, which comes from the Lord, who is the Spirit (2 Corinthians 3:17, 18).

No matter how far away from God we feel, there's no place we can go that his eye can't see, his hand can't reach, and his heart won't beckon us home. God says if we want to live happy, fulfilled lives, we must become like him whom we worship. That's why it is so important to choose to worship Jehovah God and to take him as he is.

Focus Your Faith

1. Montesquieu said, "If triangles had a god, he would have three sides." What's really wrong with shaping God into a convenient image?

2. What do you hear Christians today say about God that you do not think first-century Christians would have said?

3. What can we learn about God's image by looking at Jesus? What can we learn about our image by looking at Jesus?

4. How would you feel if your mate or best friend made a sculpture of what they *wished* you looked like, instead of the *real* you, and then spent all their time gazing at the sculpture and ignoring you?

5. How do you try to keep God "in his place" in your life? Describe three ways that you try to manipulate God for your own purposes.

6. "Whom you worship determines who you are." Who would your neighbors say *you* are by watching your home life? What/whom do they see you worshiping?

7. How does your church, as the body of Christ, reveal the true God to the world?

Chapter 5

Plotting Your Pivot Point

꙰

J enny worked in the executive offices of a bank owned and operated by a group of orthodox Jewish men in Pittsburgh, Pennsylvania. The men treated Jenny with respect, but they constantly used "Jesus Christ" as their

> ## Principle 3:
>
> ### *Respect What Is Holy*
>
> *Exodus 20:7*
> *Matthew 12:34-37*

slang and profanity. Because they were Jewish and didn't accept Jesus as the Son of God, using his name as a byword never bothered them at all. But it bothered Jenny, a Christian and daughter of an elder, a great deal.

On several occasions Jenny had mentioned to the men that she did not appreciate their use of her Lord's name in such irreverent ways. They would make some offhand apology like, "Please excuse my

French," but their habit never changed.

Finally, Jenny could not tolerate their profanity anymore. She knew she either had to make them understand her point or resign her position and get another job. One day the executives were all standing around Jenny's desk discussing business. The conversation was liberally sprinkled with their words of disrespect for Jesus. Jenny, being the employee and underling, sat quietly for a few minutes, trying to ignore the offensive language. At last, she could take it no more. So, she stood up and said to the bank president, "Mr. Stein, why don't you just say 'Damn Moses'?"

Dead silence. Jenny had finally gotten through to them because Moses is a name highly revered by the Jewish community. Jenny slowly sat back down, wondering where she would be working the next day. But an interesting thing happened. Mr. Stein finally said, "Jenny, I sincerely apologize. You have just made me realize how disrespectful we have all been to you. Please forgive us."

Jenny, relieved but still shaking, responded, "Mr. Stein, please don't misunderstand me. I accept your apology, but it's not just me that you have offended because it is not my name that you use as profanity. And it certainly isn't my forgiveness that you need, but thank you for understanding."

The men all walked away to their respective offices in complete silence, and Jenny said she never heard one of them use Jesus' name as slang again, at least in her presence, in the many years that she continued to work for them.

The truth is, most Americans haven't gotten the point that using God's name in a vulgar or profane way is dangerous. It is unacceptable to the God they profane. It is a serious character failing and a breach of God's Code of Ethics.

I wonder, though, if those of us who are Christians have really taken the time as Jenny did to help others understand this point?

The Pivot Point

I like Bob Ludwig. I've never met him, but I still like him. Bob Ludwig is an associate minister of one of the largest churches in New England, a church of several thousand. But that's not why I like him. His academic pedigree is remarkable, but that's not why I like him. I like Bob Ludwig because, though he is trained as a scholar, he chooses every Sunday to teach three year olds, and he's done it for years. Here is a man who could teach any age group any subject no matter how complicated, but he chooses to teach three year olds. If you ask Bob Ludwig why he teaches this class he will respond, "Because I love the curriculum. It's simple—just three things: God made you. God loves you. God doesn't want you to hit anybody."

I like that curriculum, too. Bob has hit on a crucial truth. You see, in people of character, God is the pivot point. He is the one given, the one unchangeable point of reference. For it is only when we know how to respond and relate to him that we can begin to see how we should interract with the people around us.

That's why God's Code of Ethics begins with two principles teaching us how to relate to him: put God first, and take God as he is. The third principle God gave his people is respect what is holy, which says literally,

> *You shall not misuse the name of the LORD your*
> *God, for the LORD will not hold anyone guiltless*
> *who misuses his name* (Exodus 20:7).

What's in a Name?

Have you ever considered the importance of
names? Parents have. They spend a great deal of
time and effort trying to select just the right name
for their children. Of course, we all know or have
heard of someone whose parents' strange sense of
humor stuck them with a name that would burden
them for life. One of our friends grew up near a
family named Fail who named their two sons Will
and Won't (names which our friend said proved
prophetic). And then there was Governor Hogg of
Texas who showed the tremendous sensitivity to
name his daughter Ima.

---

*A good name is more desirable
than great riches.*

Have you ever known parents who couldn't agree
on a name for a child? Their discussions can get
pretty tense, because people feel strongly about
names. A name means something. Some will say a
name is just a collection of sounds put together in a
certain order. In fact, as Shakespeare pointed out, "a
rose by any other name would smell as sweet." And
there is a degree to which he was right. However, in
another way he was wrong. Just ask Will Fail. A
name is more than a group of sounds that signal a
person to turn around to see who wants him. Why
are there no little boys in our churches named
Judas? Why are there no little girls named Jezebel?
We know that names do stand for something.

For example, a name can stand for a reputation.
We even have the phrase "He's making a name for
himself." The Bible says, "A good name is more
desirable than great riches; to be esteemed is better

than silver or gold" (Proverbs 22:1). Names can stand for character. We think of certain values when we think of certain names. When I say Martin Luther King, what do you think of? I think of civil rights and the right of all people, regardless of color, to be treated equally. When I say Abraham Lincoln, what do you think of? I think of leadership and of freedom. When I say Benedict Arnold, what do you think of? I think of treason and murder.

Names represent character, and they also represent authority. If I were to approach a head of state in my own name, he wouldn't give me the time of day. But if I came as an ambassador in the name of the president of the United States, he would treat me with respect, because of the authority of the name in which I came.

Names represent character, and they also represent authority.

Names were especially meaningful in biblical times. When reading the Bible, we are impressed by how many times we are told the name of a person, what it means, and why that person was given that name. This is especially true if God does the naming or the renaming. When God changed Abram's name to Abraham, and when Jesus changed Simon's name to Peter, for example, these events were significant statements about the purpose of those lives. Another instance is found in Matthew 1:21 where the angel spoke for God to Joseph in a dream and said, "She will give birth to a son, and you are to give him the name Jesus, because he will save his people from their sins."

It is also interesting to note that, in Scripture, to

name someone is to have authority and dominion over him. In Genesis, we read that God brought the animals before Adam and told him to name them. And God told Adam and Eve, "Be fruitful and increase in number; fill the earth and subdue it. Rule over the fish of the sea and the birds of the air and over every living creature that moves on the ground" (Genesis 1:28). This principle is also why God allowed Adam to give his wife the name Eve, for God ordains that the authority in the home should belong to the husband. Naming is an important thing to God. That is why it was God and not people who named the Son of God.

Have you ever been acquainted with someone whose name you don't know or have forgotten— perhaps the cashier at the grocery store, or a neighbor, or maybe even someone in your church? I call these face-to-face relationships, because I can't talk to any of these people unless we're standing face to face. I'm too embarrassed to run after them shouting, "Hey, you!" and I'm too proud to admit to someone I've been greeting for years that I couldn't call his name to save my life! That's an awkward feeling, isn't it? My tendency in those situations is to run when I see those people coming, or at least to make the encounter as brief as possible. I don't want to be found out! Either way, I'll never have a meaningful relationship with any of them until I swallow my pride and ask their names.

When God gives us his name or names, he is inviting intimacy. He is saying, "Get to know me." You see, we don't give God names. God volunteers his names to us. Anytime God reveals one of his names to us, he tells us something about his character and nature. The personal name for God, the one mentioned in the third principle, is *Yahweh*, "I AM." The most fundamental characteristic about God is

that he is. He always has been, and he always will
be. Now, what does that name tell you about God?
By revealing that name, God has told us of his
eternal nature. He's also told us of his sovereignty,
for, if he is eternal, he is over everything. His name
also indicates his faithfulness, for God does not
change. He keeps his promises. David was right
when he said, "Those who know your name will trust
in you, for you, LORD, have never forsaken those who
seek you" (Psalm 9:10). If you *really know* God's
name, understanding what it is and what it means,
you will trust him.

**When God gives us his name or
names, he is inviting intimacy.**

Consequently, God's name should never be used in
connection with a vanity. The old King James instruction not to use the LORD's name "in vain" helps
us understand something of the meaning of the
original Hebrew. The Hebrew word for "in vain" here
means something that is empty, meaningless, without substance. It is wrong to take the name of I AM,
the name that says "I never lie, I never change, I will
always be" and attach it to something with absolutely no meaning. G. Campbell Morgan was right
when he preached that men must use the name of
God in a way that is true to its meanings and its
intentions. When we misuse his name, we reveal
something about ourselves—either we don't understand the nature of God, or we just don't care about
him. There's a heartbreaking verse in Isaiah 52:5
where God is mourning the plight of his people. As
he lists the evils of that day, he says, "And all day
long my name is constantly blasphemed."

Have you ever thought about how many times each day the Holy God who made heaven and earth must hear his name blasphemed or profaned? *Profanity*, by the way, comes from two root words: *pro*, meaning "out of," and *fanum*, meaning "temple." Therefore, *profanity* literally means "out of the temple." A person profanes something when he takes a holy thing and uses it out of its holy context. Of course, when questioned, most people respond, "I didn't mean anything by it." But the point of the third principle is that we shouldn't utter God's name unless we *do* mean something by it, because his name does mean something. We must respect what is holy.

How We Misuse God's Name

Because God's name is so important, we should expect Satan to try to find ways to pervert our use of it. There are basically five different ways people misuse the name of God. The first two types represent ways we most often hear his name misused by people in the world. The last three are ways we most frequently hear it misused by those of us in the church.

1. As a Curse

This type of profanity is an example of weak people using strong words, and it's one of the most common ways people misuse God's name. Have you ever worked around someone who didn't think people took him seriously unless he attached some sort of curse word to what he was saying? With these people, the priority of their instructions is measured by the amount of vulgarity preceding and following the directions. If, for example, the task is something to do as you have free time, the person asks nicely, "I have a project for you. . . ." On the other hand, if the boss is pressing him or her for answers, it's, "Get that blankety-blank report, blank blank it!"

And we all know someone who gets angry or frustrated and asks God to damn whom- or whatever he sees as the source of his problem. What in the world could be more unholy than damning someone or something in the name of God? By the way, did you know that when we ask God to damn someone, we're demanding God to do something he's never done? John 3:17, 18 tells us that men condemn themselves when they refuse the light of the Son of God and choose darkness instead. God's name should be a blessing, not a curse.

2. As an Exclamation Point

People often use the names of the Godhead to express reactions of all sorts of emotions. I don't mean to be offensive, but let me give you some examples. A person hears some startling news and responds, "Oh my God!" Or someone sees a rather gruesome scene and under his breath whispers, "Jesus!" There was a time when this type of language would be frowned upon by society, but that is certainly not the case today. In fact, I was watching what I thought was a family TV show recently with my son Michael when, in the space of about 30 seconds, the characters in the show used God's name as an exclamation point five times. Again, they "didn't mean anything by it." They were just using God's name as a synonym for "Oh, you're kidding!" or "I can't believe that!" I decided right then that there was something better I could be doing with my son than watching that television show.

Actually, what God is saying in the third principle is that, just as the names he reveals to us tell us something about him, the way we use those names reveals much about ourselves—our character. What kind of role model, for example, did the tapes of Richard Nixon's White House conversations reveal him to be? In hours and hours of discussions, hardly a sentence could be transcribed without one of his expletives being deleted. The way we use God's name speaks volumes about us. But what does it say? For some of us, it speaks of ignorance. Quite frankly, there are people today who do not know this kind of language is offensive to God. Or, perhaps, it speaks of unbelief. After all, what does it matter how one uses the name of a god who does not exist?

The way we use God's name speaks volumes about us.

For many people, though, misusing God's name is not a sign of ignorance or disbelief, but a symptom of a lack of emotional control. We get angry and, rather than exerting a little restraint, we give our target both barrels. Of course, some professionals counsel people to vent their anger. And I've heard many explain they "just can't help it." But my experience makes me wonder a little about that excuse. I'm a golfer, and once in a while I like to show up at the golf course and join whatever group happens to be playing. It's a good way to meet people. Usually about the second or third hole, after I've heard all kinds of speech, someone in the group will ask me what I do for a living, and I'm happy to tell them that I'm a minister. Not always, but in almost all instances, I witness an amazing transformation in speech. These experiences tell me that we *can* control our speech if and when we want to. But because society (which is you and me) no longer demands it, many are no longer willing to exert the effort.

In short, our misuse of God's name reveals at a very basic level a spiritual problem. For as Jesus taught, what comes out of the mouth really comes out of the heart:

> "You brood of vipers, how can you who are evil say anything good? For out of the overflow of the heart the mouth speaks. The good man brings good things out of the good stored up in him, and the evil man brings evil things out of the evil stored up in him. But I tell you that men will have to give account on the day of judgment for every careless word they have spoken. For by your words you will be acquitted, and by your words you will be condemned" (Matthew 12:34-37).

The man we all know as Colonel Sanders, the founder of Kentucky Fried Chicken, embraced Christ late in his life, and he made the comment once that "becoming a Christian cost me half of my vocabulary." We must realize that people of character don't use God's name as a curse or as an exclamation point.

3. As a Cliché

Many of us in the church are guilty of this type of misuse, I'm afraid. It's such a good way to sound spiritual! We say, "Oh praise the Lord!" with such regularity that we don't even realize what we're saying anymore. Jesus talked about divine name-dropping in Matthew 6 when he warned us not to be people who love to pray in public, going on and on with long, showy prayers.

God's name should be used or associated only with things of substance and genuineness. His name is not a cliché, and we should not use it unless we deeply mean what we say. When we say, for example, "I believe that Jesus is Lord" and are baptized into the name of the Father, the Son, and the Holy Spirit, we are supposed to mean what we say. When bride and groom stand in the presence of the church and before the minister and pledge, "With God as my witness, I will not leave you till death do us part," they are supposed to be serious about their commitment. We're not to use God's name lightly for our own purposes. God's name is not just some designer label we wear to look good in front of our peers. We don't use it to impress people. When we use God's name lightly, we show that we take God lightly as well.

4. As a Weapon

Another way people in the church misuse the names of God is to intimidate others. In reality they are committing spiritual forgery, for they are using God's name in an unauthorized way to benefit themselves. For example, Brother So-and-so walks up, puts his arm on your shoulder, and says, "Brother, God told me to tell you . . ." And before you know what's happening, Brother So-and-so is laying out his agenda for your life. Do you see how Brother So-and-so is trying to intimidate you now by using God's name as a weapon? What can you say to him, "I'm sorry, I don't want to listen to God right now"?

Several times in my ministry, people have approached me to move to their congregation as the pulpit minister. Almost without exception, they've told me that after much prayer, they're sure it is God's will that I move. The problem is that, except for the one move I've made in my ministry, when I prayed, I did not believe God was directing me to a

new congregation. Sometimes we may confuse the
Father's wishes with those of our own.

Teachers are to bring the people a word from the
Lord. If you are a teacher, and realizing that fact
doesn't send you to your knees, perhaps you need to
stop teaching. One of the great cries of the prophets
of the Old Testament was against people who
claimed to be delivering messages from God when
they had received none. It is an awesome thing to
use the name of the Lord. We need to be sure we're
delivering his thoughts and not just our own. Don't
use his name as a weapon to intimidate others.

5. As an Endorsement

Sometimes we try to link our names with the
King of kings by using God's name for our own
personal gain. Let me give you an earthly example of
this "credibility by association" game. In the 1988
vice-presidential debate, Dan Quayle responded to a
question by likening himself to John F. Kennedy.
Lloyd Bentsen immediately rebutted, "Sir, I knew
Jack Kennedy. I worked with Jack Kennedy. And,
Senator, you are no Jack Kennedy." In this instance,
both men were playing the game.

Our society accepts the fact that association with
rich, powerful, or popular people lends credibility to
what one says or does. People often attend a celeb-
rity function so that, because of their association
with the rich and powerful, others will deem them to
be so. We don't have to do more than turn on the TV
to see how deeply association affects our thought
processes. Why else are professional athletes paid
outrageous fees to let us in on what underwear they
recommend? Or why are recording artists paid
millions to tell us which soft drinks are "cool"?

This game is not appropriate with God's name.
Even so, there are many Christians who try to play

it. That's right, Christians often "namedrop" God.
They regularly sign his name to things not worthy of
it. Some people commercialize the name of God to
sell their product. I don't believe God wants his
name marketed for people's selfish purposes. If you
are a Christian, be a Christian businessman. But I
don't know that he wants the Praise the Lord Lumber Company.

Just as some try to use God's name to sell products, others try to use his name to buy votes. In the
1980 election, both the Carter and the Reagan
campaigns kept themselves and the postal service
busy mailing out information to convince the voters
which candidate was the *most* "born again"! Both
candidates wanted the evangelical vote in November, and they believed that their association with
God would deliver that vote.

I don't believe God wants his
name marketed for people's
selfish purposes.

Perhaps at this point you're feeling pretty good
about how you use his name. I was . . . until I
started searching my own life to see if I've been
using his name to indulge myself. And I have to
admit to you I didn't come out completely clean. You
see, I've been guilty of using one of God's names to
endorse things that I want when I pray. How many
of us have prayed and invoked the holy name of our
Lord Jesus when the sole intention of that prayer
was just to get God to do something we wanted for
our own selfish purposes? James says in James 4:3,
"When you ask, you do not receive, because you ask
with wrong motives, that you may spend what you

get on your pleasures."

How We Should Use God's Name

It's an important thing to take the third principle of God's Code of Ethics seriously. It just may be that the way the church profanes the name of God is every bit as offensive to him as the profanity out on the street. Jesus said, "Many will say to me on that day, 'Lord, Lord, did we not prophesy in your name, and in your name drive out demons and perform many miracles?' " Do you see what they're saying? "Oh Lord, we used your name, we worked in your name, we served in your name!" But Jesus replies, "I never knew you. Away from me, you evildoers!" (Matthew 7:22). How should we use his name?

1. As a Claim to Authority

A good way to positively state the third principle might be "You shall take the name of the Lord your God in earnest." We should care about whether or not God's name is honored.

When Jesus taught his disciples to pray in Matthew 6:9, he began his prayer, "Our Father in heaven, hallowed be your name." Christians should not only refrain from misusing our Lord's name, but should fervently pray that all the world will recognize his name and worship him.

The missionaries in India tell a story about a man known as Brother Hyde, who was famous for his personal relationship with God. The missionaries had a meeting once and called on Brother Hyde to lead the prayer. He was silent for so long that the other missionaries began to feel uncomfortable. Had the old man not heard his name? Finally, the saintly old man spoke, but all he said was, "Oh, God." And, again, he fell silent, and this time the younger men joined him in his meditation. By his example, Brother Hyde showed these younger missionaries that using the name of God is such a holy act that it shouldn't ever be said flippantly, and must always be used reverently. As the psalm says, "Ascribe to the LORD the glory due his name; worship the LORD in the splendor of his holiness" (Psalm 29:2).

God's name carries authority. It represents the power that takes a person who has lost his direction, ruined his relationships, alienated himself from his God and from the purpose God intended for his life and remakes that lonely, broken person into a man or woman who shares the character of God. God is not only our Maker; he is also our Remaker. In religious terms, that means "Savior." Acts 4:12 says, "Salvation is found in no one else, for there is no other name under heaven given to men by which we must be saved." Paul says, "Everyone who calls on the name of the Lord will be saved" (Romans 10:13). And how do we call upon his name? In Acts 22:16, Ananias said to Saul, "What are you waiting for? Get up, be baptized and wash your sins away, calling on his name." Power! Awesome power!

2. As a Call to Integrity

There is a legend that a young soldier was once brought before Alexander the Great for punishment because the young man had been causing problems among his fellow soldiers, which was a serious offense punishable by death. "What is your name?" Alexander asked the accused. "Alexander," the boy replied. The great general, taken aback, responded, "Either change your name or change your conduct." That's good advice for Christians. The third principle is asking us if God can endorse our lives—if he would really want to sign his name to them. It may just be that he would like to say to us, as Alexander

did the boy, "Change your life or change your name."
In other words, don't call yourself "Christian" but act
like the world. Paul said, "Everyone who confesses
the name of the Lord must turn away from wickedness" (2 Timothy 2:19).

If we are to bear Christ's name, then our lives
must have a quality about them that reflects the
meaning of his name. Paul put it more clearly than I
can: "Whatever you do, whether in word or deed, do
it all in the name of the Lord Jesus, giving thanks to
God the Father through him" (Colossians 3:17).
Using God's name is a call to integrity.

3. As a Call to Intimacy

The Hebrews overreacted to the third principle
and became afraid even to pronounce the name of
God. God's concern was not our _use_ but our _misuse_ of
his name. Indeed, the very fact that he revealed his
name indicates that he wants to be known to us, and
he wants us to be able to call on him by name. Jesus
said, "My Father will give you whatever you ask in
my name" (John 16:23). He _wants_ us to use and to
wear his name because doing so will cause us to be
people of character. Honoring his name will change
us from haughty to humble, from pompous to poor in
spirit, from rebellious to respectful.

Merv Griffin once interviewed Charlton Heston
about Heston's experience playing Moses in the
movie, _The Ten Commandments_. Griffin asked,
"Charlton, has making a religious movie impacted
your spiritual outlook?"

Heston looked at Griffin and replied, "You can't
walk barefoot down Mount Sinai and be the same
person you were when you went up."

God is calling you to the summit, too. But remove
your shoes, for you are on holy ground.

Focusing Your Faith

1. Proverbs 22:1 says "a good name is more desirable than great riches." List three ways in which *your* good name is better than riches to you.

2. Many names for God are found in the Bible. Which is your favorite? Why?

3. How do you explain the frequency with which the third principle is violated? What influences people to use God's name without thinking what it means?

4. God mourned his people's lack of respect for his name (Isaiah 52:5). What emotion do you feel when you hear someone use his name disrespectfully?

5. How do you hear people misuse God's name at work? At church? How does God want us to use his name?

6. What things would you see or hear change if everyone quit using God's name with disrespect?

7. If Americans began to truly respect God's holy name, which industries would have to change? What would they have to do differently?

Chapter 6

Distress

Signals

∽

The Greeks and the Persians were at war in 490 B.C. Persian soldiers had just destroyed the Greek city of Eretria and were on the march again toward the plain of Marathon. A Greek

Principle 4:

Seek Rest with God

Exodus 20:8-11

Mark 2:27

soldier named Pheidippides ran 24 hard miles without stopping from Athens to Sparta to take the news. But as soon as he arrived and delivered his message, he dropped dead from exhaustion. He gave his life for the run. Today the famous marathon race of 26 miles commemorates his feat. And most of us in America live our lives as if we're in a life-and-death marathon race. We give our lives for the run.

When Jamie and I were first married, we were in a Sunday school class for newly married couples. We

had a wonderful teacher who had a wife and two
children. He was holding down a full-time job and a
part-time job. On top of that, he was going to school
to get a graduate degree. I can remember one Sunday he stood before the class looking rather haggard
and said with mock solemnity, "Friends, I'm tired. I
think I've been tired since the eighth grade."

"Busyness" has become the hallmark of American lifestyle.

Of course, our friend was joking, but it was hu-
morous because we had all shared that feeling. If we
polled that class today, ten years later, most of us
would agree that we have, if anything, stepped up
the pace of life since the day we laughed at that
young father's fatigue. "Busyness" has become the
hallmark of American lifestyle. But many of us
aren't laughing at the tiredness anymore. We are a
driven people—driven to excel, driven to succeed,
driven to win. It's like being on a treadmill that's set
two notches faster than we can comfortably walk.
Sometimes we ignore the distress signals our body
sends out. We can't quite keep up—at least not for
long. But the question we need to ask ourselves is,
Why? Why are we on this treadmill?

Two words summarize the lives of most Americans—hurry and worry. We hurry through our lives,
worried about what the future may hold, never
reflecting on the bigger issues of life. It's a sad thing
to visit the hospital room of a person who knows he
or she is dying and who suddenly realizes that life
has been spent being "busy," but accomplishing
nothing that really matters. It's all we can do to try
to keep our juggling act going until, one day, it's

over. The act has been canceled.

Indeed, we are a nation that's driven, and this behavior is destroying our health, our families, and our character. The stress we feel shows that we know there should be more to life, but where we find that missing ingredient is a mystery to most. Jesus came so that we could have an abundant life. There is a quality of fullness and richness in living a life of character.

One thing is certain, we can never be successful enough to provide ourselves with abundant living. We will never accomplish or accumulate enough to feel comfortable with where we are. We will only become more weary.

Two words summarize the lives of most Americans—hurry and worry.

I'm not saying it's wrong to strive to achieve. Quite the contrary. Work is a gift from God, one he bestowed in the Garden. But it's wrong to let our work demand the ultimate commitment from us. What God has said is that work is not our god. I AM is our God, and people of character live by God's fourth principle in his Code of Ethics. They seek rest with God. His principle is stated this way:

> *Remember the Sabbath day by keeping it holy.*
> *Six days you shall labor and do all your work,*
> *but the seventh day is a Sabbath to the LORD*
> *your God. On it you shall not do any work,*
> *neither you, nor your son or daughter, nor your*
> *manservant or maidservant, nor your animals,*
> *nor the alien within your gates. For in six days*
> *the LORD made the heavens and the earth, the*

*sea, and all that is in them, but he rested on the
seventh day. Therefore the* LORD *blessed the
Sabbath day and made it holy (Exodus 20:8-11).*

What's Wrong with Restlessness?

This principle of rest is important to God because
we are important to God. Refusing rest takes a
heavy toll on people. I learned something the hard
way about drivenness when I first started preaching.
It doesn't let up. It knows no end. Human striving
has no conclusion to it.

In those days I wasn't married, so I could work a
lot without abusing my family. I just abused myself.
And that's exactly what I did. I would begin every
day at 8:00 A.M. I would rarely come back to my
apartment before 10:00 at night, but the work was
never done. There was always another book to read,
another call to make, another Bible study to conduct,
another visit to be made. I counted one day and
found I had worked 49 straight days non-stop, and I
wasn't ahead. I was just tired. I was even beginning
to get bitter. I was losing my interest and my passion for my ministry. I was not following God's
fourth instruction for living.

Restlessness results in obsessive behavior. We
keep telling ourselves, "If I could just do a little
more," the job would be back on schedule, or the bills
would be up-to-date, or I'd be a cinch to get the
promotion. But this kind of thinking erodes the
character as surely as it wearies the soul. Once
achieving becomes paramount, any step that moves
us toward our achievement is justified, regardless of
what that step demands of us. We lose perspective,
too, and sacrifice relationships with our families, the
very people we claim we're trying to provide for, in
order to reach our personal goals. We neglect our

mental and physical health as well as that of the people working with or under us all in the name of success.

We fight his rest because we do not trust God to provide the abundant life he has promised.

Worst of all, we let worry eat us alive. Jesus says our character problems are merely symptoms of the underlying problem that causes us to resist rest with God. We fight his rest because we do not trust God to provide the abundant life he has promised. Jesus tells us that God is fully aware of all our needs, and worrying about them merely testifies to our failure to trust in God's power to fill our needs and his desire to meet them (Matthew 6:25-34). He also says "No one can serve two masters . . . You cannot serve both God and Money" (verse 24). In other words, we reject God's rest because we've rejected God. And rejecting God is the root of all character failure.

What's Best about Rest?

Sabbath does not mean "Saturday." It means "rest." Bear in mind that Moses said the LORD has *given* you the Sabbath. The Sabbath was a gift from God, created not for his benefit, but for ours. God knew that man needs rest from his labor, and he also knew we would resist it. That's why he included this instruction.

We see the same resistance with our children. Have you ever watched young children fight sleep? They may whine and cry; they may keep themselves busy, running and playing so that they can't fall asleep. But whatever they're doing, no matter how frenzied their efforts to stay awake, they'll insist they're not tired. I've known our kids' eyes to lose their focus, and their heads seem likely to bob right off their necks in the middle of telling me, "Daddy, I'm *not* slee . . ." There are times when the mom or dad just has to *make* a child rest.

There are also times when our Father has to make us rest, too. Perhaps this is the idea the psalmist had in mind when he wrote, "He *makes* me lie down in green pastures." Has God ever made you lie down? Think for a moment. Are there times when God has said, "That's it. I've had enough. I'm going to make you lie down." God has made me rest, and it wasn't an easy adjustment for me.

The summer and fall of 1991 was one of the most frustrating periods of my life. I had mononucleosis. There is no medicine to treat mono. All that doctors can tell people who have this disease is to rest as much as possible. When the mono was at its worst, I would come home every day about 1:00 or 2:00 P.M., lie down on the bed, and just stew. I'd lie there being angry because there were books to read and there were calls to make and there was a sermon to prepare, and on and on. I just didn't have time to relax and get well! I was a frustrated sheep resisting the call of the Good Shepherd to rest with him.

Even though we may have lost our perspective on rest, Jesus never did. Sometimes we think of Jesus as being somehow "anti-Sabbath" because of his run-ins with the Pharisees over Sabbath traditions. But Jesus observed the Sabbath completely and perfectly, and he never felt guilty about a day of rest. Such times were essential to his spiritual health. He even taught the rest principle to the men whose lives he was recharactering. Once, after his disciples returned from their first preaching tour, they gathered around Jesus "and reported to him all they had done and taught. Then, because so many people were coming and going that they did not even have a chance to eat, he said to them, 'Come with me by yourselves to a quiet place and get some rest' " (Mark 6:30, 31). In fact, rather than devaluing the Sabbath, Jesus' concern was that the Pharisees' rules had perverted this gift from God so much that they had turned a beautiful gift into a burden. By the time the Pharisees were through interpreting the Sabbath instruction, they had devised 1,521 rules on how a person could break the Sabbath. Jesus' criticism was that the Pharisees had missed the Sabbath principle entirely. They had turned the day of rest into a day so burdened by rules that a person was more exhausted at the end of the Sabbath than any other day of the week. When we really understand the fourth principle, we must step back and say, "What a wonderful God we have. He wants us to rest!"

Three Blessings of Rest

The Sabbath is meant to be three things:

1. A Safeguard

The Sabbath was given to constantly remind us that there is more to life than work. It safeguards us from abusing our families. Whatever our walk in life, the times when all the work is done and we're "caught up" are so few and far between they are almost nonexistent. If we are asking our families to wait for those rare moments before we spend time with them, we're asking them to live in an emotional desert. They don't know when the next "watering hole" will come, and even when they see one on the horizon, they quickly learn not to get their hopes up, for it is most likely a mirage.

It's uncomfortable to be so blunt, but the truth is, if we are not home enough to model our values by our presence, our families will learn our priorities by our absence. Quite a few years ago, there was a song by Harry Chapin called "Cat's in the Cradle" about a man whose son was always asking for time with him. The chorus of the song said, "The cat's in the cradle and the silver spoon, Little Boy Blue and the Man in the Moon; . . . 'When you comin' home, Dad?' 'I don't know when, but we'll get together then, Son. You know we'll have a good time then.' " As the boy grows up, he becomes less and less interested in seeking out his father. Eventually, it is the father asking the son for attention, but by then it's too late. The son has become just like him.

He built into his creation a rhythm of work and rest to safeguard those families from neglect.

The father made the same mistake so many of us make. He thought it was the time demands that were temporary and the opportunities with his loved ones that were permanent. But it is just the opposite. We can only put people—even people who love us—on hold for so long. God wants us to be people of character who have families of character. And he built into his creation a rhythm of work and rest to safeguard those families from neglect.

God also is concerned with safeguarding our subordinates. The principle says we are not to work, and our "menservants or maidservants" are not to work, either. Employers, as God's man or woman, you are to see to it, that the people who work for you are not abused in their work by ceaseless, continual labor. God made you with needs, and they have the same needs. God included these instructions protecting workers to remind employers that God is equally concerned about the well-being of all people. Whenever I think of protecting employees' days off, I think of the Chic-Fil-A chicken restaurant with outlets in malls across the nation. In spite of the fact that virtually all other businesses in the malls are open on Sunday, Truett Cathy, the owner of Chic-Fil-A, stands by his decision that Sunday will be a day of rest for his employees. In an age when the only standard that "successful" businessmen and women seem to apply is "will it make money?" this kind of sacrifice is worthy of note. It's an all-too-rare example of choosing principle over profit.

Finally, honoring the Sabbath prevents us from abusing ourselves. I am persuaded that many of us are dishonoring our bodies by the constant stress we are asking them to bear. Keeping up a frantic pace with no relief will inevitably take its toll on our bodies. In effect, we are violating God's sixth principle, "Do not kill," because we are violating the fourth principle and slowly murdering our bodies with ceaseless toil.

2. A Reminder

Dishonoring the Sabbath places high demands on our bodies, but it also takes its toll on our souls. If we gain any insights into our own nature from Old Testament history, one must surely be that humans are prone to forget . . . to forget who God is, to forget what God has done, to forget why we are here and what gives life meaning. Because God cares so much for us, he gave us the Sabbath as a time to remember this truth and to reorient our lives in view of it.

I'm told that pilots learning to fly planes in weather

with very poor visibility can experience a sensation
known as "vertigo." They cannot tell by looking out
the cockpit windows whether the plane is flying at a
level altitude or whether it is going up or down or
turning left or right. They become completely disori-
ented to where the plane is in relation to the ground,
but they may not even be aware they are experiencing this problem. The only safe way for a pilot to fly
in weather like this is to learn to look at, interpret,
and trust the plane's instruments. The pilot must
guide the plane by what the instruments tell him is
reality.

---

*Sabbath rest is not merely
refraining from work; it's refraining
from work so we can do something holy.*

Sabbath rest should be to people of character what
those instruments are to the pilot. It's a time when
we take our eyes off the confusing, misleading input
our senses are receiving from the world outside, and
we concentrate on the truths we can trust to guide
us. Part of this reorientation occurs in our private
communion with God, in prayer, praise, and the
study of his Word. But another part is available to
us only in the context of the community of believers.
    Jesus' life shows us the importance of both pri-
vate and corporate worship. How often do we read of
Jesus' rising early or staying up late to talk to the
Father alone? And Luke 4:16 gives us an insight into
Jesus' Sabbath habits as well. He returned to
Nazareth, where he'd been reared, and on the Sabbath day, he went to the synagogue "as was his
custom." If the Son of God, who was in his very
essence God, needed time alone with the Father *and*

time to worship the Father with other believers, it is difficult, indeed, to believe that we need any less. Sabbath rest is not merely refraining from work; it's refraining from work so we can do something holy. It's a reminder to keep God in our lives. It is a time when we can filter a week's propaganda through God's unchangeable principles for living a life of character.

3. A Sign

The Sabbath was to be a reminder and a safeguard to the Israelites, but it was also to be a sign to the nations. God told Moses, "Say to the Israelites, 'You must observe my Sabbaths. This will be a sign between me and you for the generations to come, so you may know that I am the LORD, who makes you holy' " (Exodus 31:13). And, what's more, God intended the Israelites to keep the Sabbath not just when it was convenient but all through the year. In Exodus 34, the Israelites are instructed to take every seventh day to rest, even in planting or harvesting seasons, because doing so demonstrated to the nations around them the difference between grasping for life and being given life by a loving Creator. It was to indicate that Israel prospered, not because of the industry of its people, but because of the blessing of its God.

Sabbath should still be just such a sign today. Do you remember the movie *Chariots of Fire?* It tells the story of Eric Liddell, son of Scottish missionaries to China. Blessed with great speed, Eric prepared for several years to represent his country and his king in the 1922 Olympic Games in Paris. On the ship crossing the Channel, however, he learned that his race would be run on Sunday, and he believed strongly that Sunday belongs only to the Lord and not to games. In the face of strong pressure from the

British Olympic Committee and the king, and in spite of the years of training for this one race, he decided he could not run. Not running might bring dishonor to himself and the king of Britain, he reasoned, but running would dishonor the King of heaven. And that he could not do. Now, you may or may not agree with his stance, but it was quite clear to the entire world that Eric Liddell had made a statement of faith about who claimed his highest allegiance.

People of character resist the temptation to compromise their values in order to secure their future.

People of character resist the temptation to compromise their values in order to secure their future. They have a lifestyle that says to onlookers, "It is *God* I trust to provide for my life." Sabbath observance raises a signal to the world that above my work, above my hobbies, above my interests, above my pursuits, there is a majestic God who has first claim on my life. Please don't misunderstand me. The fourth principle does not say, "Okay, folks. God wants to make a deal. You get six days and God gets one day." The fourth principle says, "Make one day so holy and so special to God that you and your neighbors are reminded that God should be honored all week long." Perhaps songwriter Francis Havergal said it best when he wrote, "Take my life and let it be consecrated, Lord, to Thee. Take my moments and my days. Let them flow in ceaseless praise."

Is Rest Still Blessed?

Sabbath observance is something we have put on

the back burner of our spiritual lives, if we haven't written it off entirely. But the Sabbath principle was not just thrown in with the other nine as an afterthought. In fact, it wasn't even a new idea to the Israelites any more than "Do not steal" or "Do not murder." God had spoken to the Israelites about the Sabbath earlier, when he gave instructions for the gathering of the manna he sent for their food. When some of the Israelites ignored his instructions that there would be no manna the seventh day, he said to Moses:

> "How long will you refuse to keep my commands and my instructions? Bear in mind that the LORD has given you the Sabbath; that is why on the sixth day he gives you bread for two days. Everyone is to stay where he is on the seventh day; no one is to go out." So the people rested on the seventh day (Exodus 16:28-30).

Even before Moses brought the tablets down from Mount Sinai, the people knew the Sabbath principle was important to God. But there is also reason to believe that God introduced the Sabbath principle long before Moses' time. We don't think that any of the other instructions were new to the Israelites, do we? Did the patriarchs not know it was wrong to lie or to worship other gods? The words "how long" imply that keeping the Sabbath was something the Israelites should have known to do. Perhaps they had forgotten or just neglected it, or perhaps God was reintroducing Israel to a concept they had lost in Egypt when they were slaves and were not allowed to rest every seventh day.

Remember that, in speaking of this principle, Jesus said, "The Sabbath was made for man, not

man for the Sabbath" (Mark 2:27). Jesus went past
the Mosaic command to the original purpose and will
of God for man. He implies that the Sabbath came
into being when man came into being. Jesus' reasoning, therefore, indicates that in the Sabbath there is
a principle, not just for Jews, but for all men.
People of character resist the temptation to compromise their values in order to secure their future.
The New Testament church did not bind the traditional Jewish Sabbath observance on Gentile con-
verts (Acts 15). Indeed, the fourth is the only principle of the ten that is not specifically repeated in
the New Testament. However, the New Testament
makes it clear that the early Christians realized the
importance of the principle (see Acts 20:7; 1 Corinthians 16:2). Just as the Jews on the seventh day
remembered the God who created the world, so on
the first day, Christians remember the God who is
re-creating the world through Jesus Christ.

---

*A life of faith in God provides rest—
not just for our bodies, but for our
souls as well.*

As a rule, we have discarded the day *and* the
principle that accompanied it. The principle is that
we need to set apart and hallow a specific and pro-
portionate amount of time for rest and worship. It
speaks of the quality of life God wants for his people.
A life of faith in God provides rest—not just for
our bodies, but for our souls as well. Jesus says,
"Come to me, all you who are weary and burdened,
and I will give you rest. Take my yoke upon you and
learn from me, for I am gentle and humble in heart,
and you will find rest for your souls. For my yoke is

easy and my burden is light" (Matthew 11:28-30).

Just as the Sabbath principle speaks of the kind of earthly life God has designed for people of character, it also foreshadows the eternal life he has prepared for his people. The very first Sabbath we read about was God's. As Genesis 2:2, 3 describes it, "By the seventh day God had finished the work he had been doing; so on the seventh day he rested from all his work. And God blessed the seventh day and made it holy, because on it he rested from all the work of creating that he had done." Notice that at the end of the narrative describing each of the first six days, there is the phrase, "and there was evening and there was morning—the _____ day," but there is no such closure to the description of the seventh day. Nowhere in the Bible does it say that the seventh day (and, therefore, God's rest) has ever ended. In fact, we are to be encouraged by the prospect of sharing the rest God now enjoys, for Hebrews 4:9-11 (TEV) says, "As it is, however, there still remains for God's people a rest like God's resting on the seventh day. For whoever receives that rest which God promised will rest from his own work, just as God rested from his. Let us, then, do our best to receive that rest. . . ."

That's where the problem is—in the receiving. God has given us the glorious, revitalizing gift of rest. All that's left is for us to accept it. If we don't enjoy resting with God now, do we expect to enjoy resting with him eternally? It reminds me of the old TV show called "The Millionaire." A wealthy man's courier would ring someone's doorbell and offer them a no-strings-attached cashier's check for one million dollars. All they had to do was sign for it. And that's what happened to us. God's courier, Moses, has offered us the riches of God's rest. All we have to do is receive it.

Take a Rest Test

Let's assume that you want to accept God's gift of rest. If you're like me, rest is so foreign to your way of thinking and living that it's hard to know *how* to do it. Perhaps it will be helpful to ask ourselves these questions:

Am I Refreshed?

I certainly don't want to legislate to you how you can refresh yourself. People have tried that in the past, and it doesn't work. That's one of the mistakes the Pharisees of Jesus' time made. People refresh themselves in different ways. In fact, if you've been cooped up inside all week, perhaps what you need is to go outside and do something. But, whatever you do, it should be something that equips you to go to work the next day refreshed in mind, body, and soul, so that you can honor God with your work.

A word of caution here, though. Sometimes what we do when we're "resting" is not really rest at all. We can wear ourselves out with what we call "leisure" activities. As Gordon MacDonald says in his book *Ordering Your Private World* (Oliver-Nelson Publisher):

> Leisure and amusement may be enjoyable, but they are to the private world of the individual like cotton candy to the digestive system. They provide a momentary lift, but they will not last. I am not by any means critical of the pursuit of fun-filled moments, diversion, laughter, or recreation. I am proposing that these alone will not restore the soul in the way that we crave. Although they may provide a sort of momentary rest for the body, they will not satisfy the deep need for rest within the private world.

Am I Reflective?

The difference between what we call leisure and amusement and the kind of rest God wants us to seek is that these types of "rest" rarely provide opportunities for reflection on God's goodness and for refocusing our lives. Sabbath rest means asking myself, "Am I taking time to think about the goodness of God who has delivered me?"

. . . God has built into us a need for quiet time with him, time when we are away from the noise, time when we can be still and rest and think about him."

David said, "He leads me beside quiet waters." Abraham Heschel describes the reflective nature of Sabbath rest this way: "It is a day on which we are called upon to share what is eternal in time, to turn from the results of creation to the mystery of creation; from the world of creation to the creation of the world. God has built into us a need for quiet time with him, time when we are away from the noise, time when we can be still and rest and think about him."

Am I Refocused?

Once, in the midst of the Watergate trials, Judge John Scirica asked Jeb McGruder how he could enter into something that seemed so clearly wrong. McGruder replied, "Sir, somewhere along the line I lost my moral compass, and with it, the ability to navigate my life." I believe that Jeb McGruder put his finger right on the mark in terms of explaining the condition of people who do not regularly stop to examine and evaluate the focus of their lives—they lose their moral compass. People of character take time to regularly meet with God and with other Christians to check their compass reading—to get back in line with true values and absolute realities.

Rest is a gift, but, to receive it, we must trust the Giver! Taking time to know and trust him is what Sabbath rest is all about. Actually, knowing and trusting God is what the first four principles are about. Putting God first, taking God as he is, respecting what is holy, and seeking rest with him are the only places we can start building the life of character that we desire.

The quest for character begins with God. And it is the only pursuit that replaces constant exhaustion with permanent exhilaration.

Focusing Your Faith

1. Why are most Americans so driven? Would you describe yourself as a "driven" person in relation to your work? Why?

2. Have you ever experienced burnout? What appropriate Bible passage has helped you?

3. When you hear Jesus whisper to you, "Come with me by yourself to a quiet place and get some rest" (Mark 6:30), what do you usually say to him in response?

4. Has God ever had to "make you lie down"? Describe the experience.

5. What other cultures take rest more seriously than we do? What do Americans typically think of those people?

6. If a new Christian asked you if she should continue in a job that required her to work on Sundays, under what circumstances would you say yes? Under what circumstances would you say no?

7. Analyze the difference between being "busy" for God and being "productive" for God.

Chapter 7

Not at the White House But at *Your* House

∽

The Brothers Grimm tell a fairy tale about a father, a mother, a little boy, and the father's old father, who lived with them. The old man was feeble and his hands shook, and mealtimes could be especially trying because he often spilled his food or let it run out the corners of his mouth.

> **Principle 5:**
>
> *Make Family a Priority*
>
> *Exodus 20:12*
> *Colossians 3:18-21*

These mealtime mishaps became more and more annoying to the mother until one day the old man turned over a bowl of soup and she said, "I've had it. A meal is a time to rest and enjoy, not a time to watch someone make a mess every night." So she fixed a little table over in the corner with a little wooden bowl and said, "From now on, you eat over there." And he did. He would get up every now and then and look toward the table, but he never said a word.

A few weeks later, he spilled some food over in his corner and got it all over the floor. His daughter-in-law shrieked, "If you're going to eat like a pig, you're going to eat out of a pig's trough!" So they got a little trough, stuck his food in it, and told him to eat out of it. So, he did.

A few days later their little boy was out in the backyard. It was suppertime, and the dad went out to get him. The boy was playing with a hammer, some nails, and some wood. The dad asked, "Son, what are you doing?" The little boy looked up and said, "I'm making a trough for you and Mommy for when you get old." The father went in that very night and brought his dad back to the table.

America's ambassador to Japan, Douglas MacArthur II, served as Counselor of the State Department under John Foster Dulles. Like Dulles, MacArthur was a hard worker. Once when Dulles telephoned the MacArthur home asking for Doug, Mrs. MacArthur mistook him for an aide and snapped irately, "MacArthur is where MacArthur always is, weekdays, Saturdays, Sundays, and nights—*in that office!*"

Within minutes, MacArthur got a telephone order from Dulles: "Go home at once, boy. Your home front is crumbling." The character crisis in America hits closest to home *at* home.

The home front *is* crumbling. As Curtis Jones said, "There is a crisis in America as crucial as civil rights, dangerous as bureaucracy, insidious as communism, unpredictable as politics, uncontrollable as inflation. It is the erosion of the home."

The violence taking place in homes across America is overwhelming. You may have been a victim of that violence. When we think about this violence, we

usually think about it as being aimed at children.
But that's not the whole story. Sometimes children
themselves are the perpetrators of the violence. In
fact, approximately eight million parents in the
United States are physically abused by their children every year. And that estimate does not include
the mental abuse that goes with living in a culture
that rejects age and idolizes youth.

_Approximately eight million parents in
the United States are physically abused
by their children every year._

We seem especially fond of the game in which we try
to appear to align ourselves with his instructions
when we are actually taking his principles and
broadening them into standards that are too vague
to apply to general living. People have taken the
fifth principle, for example, and said that it means
we have a _collective_ responsibility to the elderly.
Therefore, we pay our taxes so they can receive their
Social Security benefits. On special holidays we
make fruit baskets and take them to the nursing
home. Jesus was upset with the Pharisees for playing this game. They attempted to shirk their responsibility to provide for their aging parents by saying
their property was dedicated to God and was, therefore, unavailable for their parents' use (Mark 7:9-13).
   It takes more than lip service and mind games to
take hold of the quality of life God desires for his
people of character. We can try to "beat the system"
by appearing religious while actually pursuing our
own self-interested goals. But, as we've already seen,
character comes from a commitment on the inside to
honor God and to live honorably with those he's

placed around us. God wants us to honor our own parents.

The family is the setting God has designed for children to learn the core values of life that develop character. As Jonathan Edwards explained, "Every Christian home ought to be, as it were, a little church, consecrated to Christ, and wholly influenced and governed by his rules." That's why God's ethic says the birthplace for developing character, the training ground for learning God's values, is the home. And the starting point in the home is learning to honor parents. In Exodus 20:12 God says, *Honor your father and your mother, so that you may live long in the land the LORD your God is giving you.* A nation is without character when it fails to give honor to whom honor is due. And the fifth principle in God's Code of Ethics for recharactering his people says God thinks honor is due our parents.

Principles of Honor

An Entitled Right

We tend to honor people who we think earn it— athletes, politicians, successful people. God says we are to honor parents not because of what they've done, but for who they are.

God says we are to honor parents not because of what they've done, but for who they are.

When I go into a court of law, I call the judge "Your Honor." I may not like his personality, but I honor him because of his position. The instruction does not say to honor parents' mistakes. It does not say to honor their sins. But it does say to honor their position as authorities in the home.

Jesus himself lived this way. The very Son of God "went down to Nazareth with [his parents] and was obedient to them" (Luke 2:51). The Son of God honored the position that God had given to his earthly parents.

In fact, the Bible says that parents are placed over children by God's design. Romans 1:30 and 2 Timothy 3:2 both contain long lists of terrible sins that are an affront to God, and in the midst of both these lists of horrible sins, there is the phrase "disrespectful to their parents." Perhaps seeing how seriously God takes dishonoring parents helps us understand why for centuries the Jews have said the fifth principle belongs with the first four. To their way of thinking, if parents are by God's ordination his spokesmen for children on earth, then to disrespect parents is to disrespect God.

In other words, God wants us to honor parents because they are representatives of him. This is a concept that Jamie and I have tried hard to instill in our children: that if they do not learn to respect and obey us, their earthly parents, it will always be difficult for them to respect and obey the Heavenly Father.

A Social Matter

Israel regarded disobedience to parents as a social offense calling for a community response. Today, we handle things differently. We think our kids' actions are the family's business and no one else's. One of the quickest ways to make somebody really angry is to confront them about the behavior of their kids.

However, Deuteronomy 21 makes it clear that in Bible times people regarded disrespectful and rebellious children as a problem for the whole society, a problem the whole society must address. God taught the Israelites that the family is the foundational unit for a godly society. If a child does not learn to respect his own home, he's unlikely to respect somebody else's life, wife, property, or reputation. Suppose today's church took the same sort of collective responsibility for children that Israel did. What a difference it could make!

Practice of Honor

God is telling us in the fifth principle that if there is no respect at home, there will be none anywhere. Barbara Bush once said, "Success does not depend on what happens at the White House, but what happens at *your* house." People have devised a lot of interesting ways of playing games with God's plan. To be people of character, we must honor our parents. But exactly what does honoring them involve?

Respect Their Role

The Hebrew word for "honor" carries the thought of "weightiness." In other words, the Hebrews felt that to honor people is to respect them as people who carry a great deal of weight in your life. In a child's case, it means to respect a parent's God-ordained function and the authority that accompanies it. By the way, do you know what is supposed to be the primary function of parents . . . what it is we should respect most about their role? They are appointed by God to be our teachers and guides. Psalm 78:5-7 says,

> He decreed statutes for Jacob and established the law in Israel, which he commanded our forefathers to teach their children, so the next **generation would know them**, even the children

yet to be born, and they in turn would tell their children. Then they would put their trust in God and would not forget his deeds but would keep his commands.

A parent's honor is based on his office as a spokesman for God, the teller of God's story and the teacher of God's law. The parent's role should be to initiate faith in the home, and that role should be respected.

Value Their Advice

One way in which we honor our parents is by valuing their advice. Proverbs 13:1 says, "A wise son heeds his father's instruction." That's not always easy to do because at least for the last three or four decades, people in this country have been raised to disrespect authority and to rebel against institutionalism. In fact, I was a victim of it.

I went through a period, like most young people in a culture that doesn't esteem authority figures, when I had a hard time heeding my parents' counsel. But an incredible thing happened when I left home for college. I went to school, but, amazingly, it was my parents who got smarter! No, they didn't take self-improvement courses or anything like that. In fact, they probably didn't change at all. But trying to live on my own taught me that these two dear people had acquired through their lives a wisdom that I should have been listening to all along.

God is very clear and complete in his plans for children. For instance, he instructs, "Children, obey your parents in everything, for this pleases the Lord" (Colossians 3:20). And the Living Bible translates Ephesians 6:1, "Children, obey your parents; this is the right thing to do because God has placed them in authority over you."

Here, too, we must to realize the importance of teaching children to obey their parents, even when the children don't understand or perhaps don't agree with their parents' instructions. It's important because there will be times in their adult lives when following God's plan will not, in their human understanding, seem best. So parents must develop in their children the habit of obeying simply out of faith in the one who instructs. Then it will be much more difficult for Satan to convince the adult children to trust their own judgment rather than God's. As people of character, we are called to give honor to our parents by trusting their wisdom and their experience—by valuing their advice.

Meet Their Needs

A third way in which we are to honor our parents is by meeting their needs. Proverbs 19:26 says, "He who robs his father and drives out his mother is a son who brings shame and disgrace." Also, Paul wrote, "If a widow has children or grandchildren, these should learn first of all to put their religion into practice by caring for their own family and so repaying their parents and grandparents, for this is pleasing to God" (1 Timothy 5:4).

This does not mean that it is wrong to participate in social programs provided by the government, but it does mean that God always intended for the family to be the chief agency by which the needs of individuals are met. It is not primarily your job or the government's job to care for those who cared for me when I was young. It is my responsibility.

An example of Jesus' provision for his mother's needs is one of the most poignant moments ever recorded. Hanging on the cross, dying, Jesus looked down at his disciple and best friend, John, and he asked John to care for Mary as though she were

John's own mother (John 19:26, 27).

One of the things that God's principle is warning us to guard against is the tendency in our world to call nonproductive people insignificant. In an agricultural society, such as ancient Israel, for example, children were of value, for they could help in the fields. But what about those old people? They couldn't work anymore. God, however, says don't measure the worth of a human being by how much he or she can produce. When our parents need our help, we honor God by meeting their needs.

Affirm Their Efforts

There is a popular trend today in secular counseling to blame all a person's problems on the mistakes of his or her parents. "You can't help the way you are," the thinking goes. "It's not your fault. Your parents messed you up."

---

*We should make our parents
feel treasured.*

Certainly, the Bible does not say that parents are perfect. And our honoring of parents is not based on how much we approve of the job they did with us. God is saying that we should make our parents feel treasured because of what they tried or are trying to do. One thing that is teaching me to honor my parents' efforts is being a parent myself. This is the hardest job I've ever had. It's hard and it's costly. The cost isn't just in terms of finances, but of time, energy, plans, and dreams. If we can honor our parents for nothing else, we can honor them because they took on a hard and costly job, and they tried.

Maybe we could restate the principle to say, "We

should treat our parents, flaws and all, as we want our children to treat us." I love the way the Today's English Version translates Proverbs 23:22: "When your mother is old, show her your appreciation."

One group of people who need all the appreciation and encouragement they can get is single parents. Being a parent has convinced me of two things: (1) Ideally, parents need to be young, because it's too exhausting to be old and have kids; and (2) Ideally, it's a two-person job. Sometimes I wonder how Jamie and I are going to make it, but when I think of the single parents in our churches who are raising godly kids without a partner, my reaction is one of awe and respect. If you are the child of a single-parent home, you should give that mother or father double honor for what they are trying to do. And the rest of us need to hold up the hands of the single-parent families and help them walk along their journey.

Forgive Their Failings

I believe the things I've said are true, and I trust they've honored God. But I want you to know that I'm aware that some of you reading this are in real pain, maybe guilt, maybe anger, maybe a little of both, because you have been deeply wounded by your parents. Some of you grew up in homes where terrible evils and horrible sins were committed against you by the very people to whom God entrusted your safekeeping. God is not saying here, "Just get over it. Ignore the pain, and deny that it ever happened." Perhaps for you this instruction is a call, if possible, to confront your parents and to discuss your pain in the hope that you can work through it together. In doing so you can be free to authentically honor your parents in the years ahead.

For some of you, confrontation and reconciliation are not possible, for your parents are dead or unwill-

ing to accept responsibility for their sins against you.
If this is your case, let me encourage you to pray.
Pray that you will not allow bitterness to control
your life, that you can forgive those who hurt you,
and that you won't continue the cycle of pain by
inflicting on your children what was visited on you. I
encourage you to pray, as well, that somehow your
pain will drive you closer to God. As David said,
"Though my father and mother may forsake me, the
LORD will receive me" (Psalm 27:10).

A Word to Parents: Be Honorable

One last word—a challenge, really—to us as
people who want to be parents of character: Be
honorable. Even though our honor isn't based on our
worthiness, we still need to live a life that makes it
easy for our children to honor us. We are to be
teachers of what is right and true about life. And we
are most true to our calling when we teach our
children the values that build character and the God
that defines those values. If we take our role as
God's authority in the home seriously, we have
reason to hope that when our children leave home
they, too, will choose to be people of character—to
act justly and to love mercy and to walk humbly
with their God.

Too often, though, we are deceived into thinking
the day-to-day opportunities we have with our
children are unimportant. James Boswell, the famous biographer of Samuel Johnson, often told a
story about a day when he was a boy that his dad
took him fishing. He always remembered the things
he and his dad talked about, all the lessons his dad
taught, and the wisdom he passed on. That single
day profoundly impacted the rest of his life. Years
later, someone found the journal that Boswell's

father kept and thought it would be interesting to
look up that very influential day. There was only one
sentence in the father's diary that day, and it said,
"Gone fishing today with my son; a day wasted." God
says to parents, "These commandments that I give
you today are to be upon your hearts. Impress them
on your children. Talk about them when you sit at
home and when you walk along the road, when you
lie down and when you get up" (Deuteronomy 6:6, 7).
Perhaps we should add "and when you're fishing."
Parents, be honorable by accepting God's ordained
role for you as teacher and guide to your children.
Model for your children God's uncompromised values
and his unquestioned integrity and unconditional
love. Teach them to trust him completely. In other
words, be honorable.

A Word to All: Value Family

The heart of the fifth principle is this: People of
character make family a priority. It's a rather som-
ber fact of life that neither children nor parents are
around for long. Someday those children won't be in
your home, and someday those parents will be gone
as well. Life is too short and the price is too high to
put off the honoring for another day. Value your
family and make them a priority.

The family that centers itself on God's design will
be a training ground for the development of character. Henry Drummond said, "Strength of character
may be acquired at work, but beauty of character is
learned at home. . . . The family is the supreme
conductor of Christianity." It will be a place where
children are taught in an atmosphere of love that, to
live a life of abundance, they must love and honor
God. And the way they start learning to love a
Father in heaven they cannot see is to learn to love

and respect the parents that they do see.

Maybe we were taught this lesson by our earthly parents, or maybe it's something God has helped us understand in spite of them. It is, nevertheless, part of his plan for recharactering us into his image.

Perhaps it comes down to the story of my friend Mary, who remembers her mother's wise words. When Mary would leave the house on a date or some other activity, her mother would say, "Don't forget whose name you're wearing." Mary says she was never sure whether her mom was talking about her father's name or her Father's name. She decided, though, that it didn't really matter because she wanted to behave in a way that would honor both of them.

Focusing Your Faith

1. What is your emotional reaction when you hear a child being disrespectful to his/her parents?

2. Would you say that children are most often disrespectful because *they* lack honor or because their parents do not require honor from them?

3. "A wise son heeds his father's instruction" (Psalm 13:1). What trends and events in society have caused us to ignore this good advice?

4. Under what circumstances should a child ever disobey his parents? Have you ever experienced one of these times?

5. What if the church today took the same sort of collective responsibility for children that the Israelites did? What problems would we see reduced? How can the church do this?

6. Compared to work, would you say you make your family a priority?

7. James Boswell's father wrote in his diary, "Gone fishing today with my son; a day wasted." Why was James's perception of the day so different? Plan a memory-making "wasted day" with a member of your family.

Chapter 8

America:
A War Zone

John Briggs and
Jeff Harbin were on
their way home to
McAlister, Oklahoma,
from Tulsa. About
sixteen miles north of
McAlister they swerved
to miss something in
the highway. Then they

Principle 6:

Respect Human Life

Exodus 20:13
1 John 3:11-18

stopped. At first they thought it was a dead animal.
Walking back toward the crumpled figure, they
stopped in horror when they found a man with blood
splattered everywhere.

Richard Taylor had been shot five times by a
criminal "friend" and left for dead. What was left of
his miserable life of crime was slowly oozing out on
the pavement, leaving a blood-red trail. He was
dying. His friends thought they had murdered him.

Hooked on heroin, Richard Taylor was guilty of a

myriad of habit-supporting crimes—armed robbery, forged checks, jumping bail—and was suspected of every other kind of mayhem, including murder. He probably deserved to die, according to the law.

But Richard Taylor didn't die. He survived. And during his recovery in the hospital and later in prison he grew to know God—the great rebuilder of shattered character. Richard gave up his worship of the mind-and-soul-control god—heroin. He began to worship the mind-and-soul-enabler God—Jehovah.

After his release from prison, he became a youth minister, preacher, and speaker to high school students around the country. He used his own story from misery to victory to inspire young people to respect human life. He brought many people out of the slums of drug abuse into the mansions of heaven. He lived the rest of his life as a man of great character—godly character.

Richard Taylor is dead now. The lack of respect he had shown his body and the physical punishment he gave it during his religion of drugs were too much for him to live a long life. But he will be remembered as a man of great character, not a man of failed character. I know because he was a member of the church where I now preach.

Richard Taylor is just one example of how America is fast becoming a war zone. Our nightly news broadcasts and morning newspapers are filled with the grisly accounts of one murder after another. Recently, a woman was convicted of hiring a "hit man" to murder the mother of her daughter's rival for a cheerleading position at school. She hoped the woman's daughter would be too upset to compete. A couple in the town where I live was just convicted of starving their teenage son to death as a form of punishment. Not long ago, a man drove his pickup truck into a small-town Luby's Cafeteria and shot to death twenty-three people, then turned the gun on himself. No one knows why. And the stories just go on and on. The sad truth is, statistically speaking, living in one of America's major cities puts us in greater danger of being killed than the soldiers who fought in the Persian Gulf War.

But murder is not just a modern problem. In fact, the first person who ever died on this planet was murdered. The first funeral on earth was not for an aged father but for a young son. And, just as it did then, murder still breaks the Father's heart today.

God puts the shortest of the principles for living quite simply, *"You shall not murder"* (Exodus 20:13). People of character respect human life. My guess is that very few of you have ever actually taken another person's life, but I'd like you to take a closer look at the sixth principle, for it involves more than just *not* doing something. And I'd like to challenge you to wait just a moment before you decide how much you need this word from God.

Behind the Principle

Let me share with you two reasons that are behind this principle. The first reason for the sixth principle is that murder steals God's sovereign right to control the world. Hebrews 9:27 says "Man is destined to die once, and after that to face judgment." And since God alone is judge, God alone should determine the court appointment. If there is a right time for a person to die, God alone must decide when that time is. The right to end life should be reserved for him who gives life.

A second reason for the sixth principle concerns the sacredness of people. In Genesis 9, Noah and his family are leaving the ark, and God is giving them rules for living in this new world washed clean by the flood. He explains to them that for the first time man will be allowed to kill animals and eat them for food. But then he says that man must not eat meat that has its lifeblood still in it, and God adds,

> "For your lifeblood I will surely demand an accounting. I will demand an accounting from every animal. And from each man, too, I will demand an accounting for the life of his fellow man.
>
> "Whoever sheds the blood of man, by man shall his blood be shed; for in the image of God has God made man" (Genesis 9:5, 6).

From the very beginning, God declared that no one has the right to number another person's days. And did you notice God's reasoning? He said, "For in the image of God has God made man." We have permission to take life from everything God created except people. God has invested a part of himself in us, and killing a person is striking at God himself.

The Principle Examined

God bases his instruction, then, on the sovereignty of himself and the sacredness of persons. But let's be more specific about what it is God is addressing here. In Hebrew, the word for "kill" means a malicious and unlawful killing, and I think the NIV has done well to translate it "murder." In the law of Moses, different types of killings are discussed.

Premeditated murder is described in Numbers 35:20, 21 where God says, "If anyone with malice aforethought shoves another or throws something at him intentionally so that he dies or if in hostility he hits him with his fist so that he dies, that person shall be put to death; he is a murderer."

Accidental homicide was a second type of killing described in the law of Moses. Numbers 35 goes on to explain this situation as one person without hostility or intent accidentally killing another. Such a killing was not a violation of the sixth principle.

Justifiable homicide describes a case in which one person is attacking another, and the defender kills the attacker to save his own life. According to the law of Moses, this type of murder does not fall under the sixth principle: "If a thief is caught breaking in and is struck so that he dies, the defender is not guilty of bloodshed" (Exodus 22:2). I believe this exception applies especially to those in society whose task is to defend people from those who would do violence to the innocent. The best application of this exception that I'm aware of is police officers. These people risk their lives every day to protect those of us who follow society's laws from those who do not. God says never to be life stealers, but he does allow people to be life defenders.

Killing in war is another type of killing that God does not condemn under the sixth principle. Certainly, there will be people who take issue with me on this opinion, but the Bible is clear that the same God who told the Hebrews not to kill often sent them into war. And in Scripture—whether it be where it tells about the soldiers who approached John the Baptist or about the soldier Cornelius—nowhere are soldiers told to give up their military careers in order to be faithful to God.

Wars are inevitable. And we may even have to become involved ourselves. But despite the conflicts going on around us, we can always strive to be people of peace.

Capital punishment is one more exception to the sixth principle. Exodus 21:12 says, "Anyone who

strikes a man and kills him shall surely be put to
death." Both Jesus and Paul, when they were
brought before the state, denied the charges brought
against them, yet they acknowledged the right of the
state to execute the death penalty. And Romans
13:1-4 makes it clear that the authority of govern-
ments to punish wrongdoers comes from God.

An Act or Attitude?

What, then, does God forbid in this sixth principle
for living? Obviously, it forbids murder. God does not
condone the theft of a life. But exactly what practices fall under the umbrella of "murder" is a matter
of rather widespread controversy today. I interpret
murder as anything that contributes to the erosion
in our society of the sacredness of the person. Con-
versely, I endorse practices that contribute to the
sacredness of the person because of the image of the
one who made us. In our decisions about how to
treat others' lives as well as in anything else, people
of character look to God as the moral center.

Most of us feel pretty good about this instruction
for living, for few of us have ever been accused of
murder. But just as not all killings are murders, not
all murders are killings—at least not in the physical
sense.

Murder is an act, but it's also an attitude. It's a
deed, but it's also a motive. Notice Jesus' interpreta-
tion of the sixth principle:

> "You have heard that it was said to the people
> long ago, 'Do not murder, and anyone who
> murders will be subject to judgment.' But I tell
> you that anyone who is angry with his brother
> will be subject to judgment. Again, anyone who
> says to his brother, 'Raca,' is answerable to the

Sanhedrin. But anyone who says, 'You fool!'
will be in danger of the fire of hell" (Matthew
5:21, 22).

Those are powerful words and convicting words, as
well. What Jesus is saying is that he knows that our
society is driven by vendettas. That's not news to us,
either, is it?

---

*Murder is an act, but it's also an
attitude. It's a deed, but it's also a
motive.*

There's an old story about a woman who is bitten
by a dog. When she goes to the doctor, the doctor
tells her the dog had rabies, and she will have to
begin treatments immediately. She, however, takes
out a pen and paper and begins making a long list of
names. "Madam," the doctor says, "we have a treatment for you. There's no need to make out a will." To
which the woman replies, "Oh, this is not a will. It's
a list of all the people I intend to bite."

That's our culture, isn't it? The other day, I saw a
bumper sticker that pretty well sums up our attitudes toward those who wrong us. It read, "Go ahead
and hit me. My daughter's a lawyer." In other words,
"You strike me, I'll strike you back harder." And
even if we exert enough control over ourselves to
resist striking back, we harbor so much bitterness in
our hearts that whoever wronged us will never get a
true kindness from us again.

I don't have to physically end your life to harbor in
my heart the attitudes that foster all of the killings
that are going on in the world. The apostle John
writes:

> This is the message you heard from the begin-
> ning: We should love one another. Do not be
> like Cain, who belonged to the evil one and
> murdered his brother. And why did he murder
> him? Because his own actions were evil and his
> brother's were righteous. Do not be surprised,
> my brothers, if the world hates you. We know
> that we have passed from death to life, because
> we love our brothers. Anyone who does not love
> remains in death. Anyone who hates his brother
> is a murderer, and you know that no murderer
> has eternal life in him (1 John 3:11-15).

You cannot be a person of character while harboring
anger and hatred.

---

*Living by his principle means going a
step further; it means actively doing
something for the good of those people
because to God they are sacred.*

If murder can be an attitude, then surely indifference can be murder. I believe that the sixth principle
forbids indifference. In other words, living by God's
plan is more than simply *not* doing evil to those
around us. Living by his principle means going a
step further; it means actively doing something for
the good of those people *because* to God they are
sacred.

If a Christian is a landlord, for example, he has the
responsibility to keep his properties in accordance
with safety codes. The welfare of his tenants should
be a greater concern to him than saving a few extra
dollars. And if a Christian sees someone hungry,
cold, poor, or homeless, he should help that person

because the poor and disadvantaged people are stamped with God's image, too. This principle is a call for you and me to support and to protect the right of every human being to live.

Ever since I came across the story of Martin Niemoller, I've been haunted by it. Niemoller was a minister of a church in Germany in the 1930s. Eventually, Niemoller became one of the millions of victims arrested and killed in Hitler's concentration camps, but before he died, he wrote:

> In Germany they first came for the Communists, and I didn't speak up because I wasn't a Communist. Then they came for the Jews, and I didn't speak up because I wasn't a Jew. Then they came for the trade unionists, and I didn't speak up because I wasn't a trade unionist. Then they came for the Catholics, and I didn't speak up because I was a Protestant. And then they came for me, and by that time no one was left to speak up.

Niemoller learned too late that indifference kills. Perhaps, if he had spoken up when Hitler's atrocities first began, his could have been the voice that made a difference.

Jesus rejected people who *thought* they'd lived lives of character because, as he said, he was hungry and thirsty, yet they gave him no food or drink, and he was naked, yet they gave him no clothes (Matthew 25:41-43). We can murder by arranging a death, or we can murder by allowing a death—by being indifferent to our fellow man. John says,

> This is how we know what love is: Jesus Christ laid down his life for us. And we ought to lay

down our lives for our brothers. If anyone has
material possessions and sees his brother in
need but has no pity on him, how can the love
of God be in him? Dear children, let us not love
with words or tongue but with actions and in
truth (1 John 3:16-18).

That New Testament passage really sums up the
sixth principle.

Beneath the Principle

How many of us can honestly say we've never
violated the sixth principle? If God is truly going to
be our moral center, we must admit our struggle to
obey in action and attitude and open our lives to his
Holy Spirit for recharactering.

**People of character value nurturing and
forgiveness.** Caring—letting people know that
because they matter to the Creator, they matter to
us—is a wonderful remedy for a world that says,
"Shoot first and ask questions later."

Do you know people who embody the real meaning
of the sixth principle? I know quite a few. They
inspire me, and sometimes their examples rebuke
me as well. They are all people of character whose
love for God calls them to seek opportunities to
nurture life.

One lady I know has kept over 100 foster children
in her home. Then there are the individuals in our
church who give their time to lead support groups
for people dealing with grief, divorce, or addictive
habits. What about the people who volunteer at food
banks and soup kitchens to feed the hungry? Or the
ladies I know who work with abused women and
children? How about those who minister to people
with AIDS, sharing the love of Christ rather than a

condescending judgment with them? My wife and I are especially thankful for the two women who chose to carry their pregnancies to term, then allowed their babies to be placed in a Christian home. What a powerful statement for life they made by their choice! And what a blessing Michael and Morgan have been to our lives! There are countless ways those of us who put God first can honor his instructions to respect human life! God is calling us to be people who choose to bless lives rather than steal them.

---

*Only when God counts for everything
does man count for anything.*

People of character respect human life.
Modern man has put God to death, and now he can't stop the killing. Our attitude toward killing is determined by our fundamental belief about what human life is in terms of its ultimate relationship, and as our society's belief in God as Creator has declined, murder has become epidemic. In short, we will never be able to live up to God's sixth principle until we start honoring his first: that we have no gods except the God of heaven and earth. Only when God counts for everything does man count for anything.

Focusing Your Faith

1. Since we are made in God's image, what are the implications for how we treat others?

2. Give examples of ways we love mankind but can't stand people. Think of a person you can't stand and decide how you will love him.

3. Compared to twenty years ago, how strongly do Americans emotionally react to the news of murder today?

4. What is happening around you to keep you from seeing that all people are sacred?

5. What billboards, ads, and movies do you see that show America's lack of respect for human life?

6. How do you apply the sixth principle to homelessness? Poverty? Racism? Euthanasia? Abortion?

7. If you personally began to show complete respect for human life, yours included, how would your life change?

Chapter 9

Flirting
with Danger

∞

In northern Europe, there is an animal called the ermine that has a snowy white fur which the animal values dearly. The ermine will do anything to keep its beautiful coat clean. In fact,

Principle 7:

Keep Sex Sacred

Exodus 20:14
Matthew 5:27, 28

when hunters find an ermine's lair, they dab the entrance with tar, then use their dogs to track the animal and chase it back to its den. When the ermine sees the tar, rather than entering its den of safety but soiling its fur, it turns and faces the dogs. Then, while the dogs hold it at bay, the hunters are able to trap it. To the ermine, purity is dearer than life. The same is true with people of character.

Sadly, most Americans no longer value purity. And the sacredness of sex is one of the primary areas that suffers as a result. Examples of the effects of our perversions of God's design for our sexuality come easily to all our minds: athletes like Magic Johnson and entertainers like Rock Hudson whose promiscuous lifestyles have brought them in contact with the AIDS virus, or so many babies being conceived out of wedlock that the "right" to have an abortion has become one of the hottest political and constitutional issues in the United States.

Studies show that 90 percent or *more* of sex portrayed on television is between people who are not married to each other. It's not really surprising that someone has said, "It is always 'sex o'clock' in America." Many of us do not need to look to the national scene or even the television set to see the effects of our society's attitude about sex. We have felt them all too personally. Research indicates that 70 percent of husbands and 50 percent of wives in America have had sex with someone beside their current spouse. The latest Janus Report indicates that as many as 35 percent of men and 26 percent of women claim to have had an extramarital affair. All too many of us have been touched by the effects of "cheap" sex.

The entertainment industry glorifies "recreational" sex, the news media reports on "casual" sex, and superstars advocate "safe" sex. But who ever speaks up for "sacred" sex? God does. In Exodus 20:14, God says, *You shall not commit adultery*. He wants us to keep sex sacred.

Many people think God and Scripture are antisex. But nothing could be further from the truth. The Bible is not prudish about human sexuality. In fact, it devotes one entire book to the subject of physical love: the Song of Solomon, which is quite graphic in its celebration of the beauty of sexual love.

A Call to Fidelity

God designed man and woman for each other. But Satan has deceived our whole society so completely that we have almost completely lost touch with any sense of what God originally intended sex to be.

A recent issue of *Newsweek*, for example, related an incident that occurred on a crowded London train. It seems a couple boarded the train at one stop and, as the train proceeded, began performing certain sex acts on each other, while the other passengers calmly kept right on reading their newspapers. When the amorous riders were through with their "lovemaking", they had the audacity to light up cigarettes inside the train. *This*, however, was too much for their fellow passengers, who loudly complained to the conductor that this was a *nonsmoking* train!

When people reach the point that they are more offended by public smoking than public sex, it's *past* time to look again at God's design for human sexuality. The Lord does not view sex as something secretive, but he does view sex as something sacred. And so do his people of character. Three important truths support God's seventh principle for living:

1. At the heart of the principle is the sacredness of marriage. God wants sex kept sacred because marriage is sacred to God, and he has a very specific purpose for sex in marriage.

The propaganda surrounding us is overwhelmingly against fidelity in marriage. Walking through an airport newsstand one day, I was attracted by the cover of a trendy women's magazine. The lead article was entitled "Ten Reasons to Commit Adultery." I thought I'd better take a look to see what the world says I'm missing, so I picked up the magazine and flipped through it to learn these ten reasons to commit adultery. One of these was, of course, that adultery is exciting. Another was that adultery makes you a well-rounded person because it gives you a wider variety of experiences. But the tenth reason was the most honest. It said you should commit adultery because adultery is fun. And isn't that the only reason to do anything?

> *The Bible defines adultery as* anything *that violates a marriage.*

Our culture might agree with *portions* of God's plan. For example, if we are going to have a decent society, we have to agree that "You shall not kill." And we also need to agree that "You shall not steal." But when we start talking about sexual values, the culture stands up and says, "Wait a second! That's not a public concern. That is a private affair."

What our culture doesn't seem to understand, is that any ethic that is going to support a society must support its families, for society is essentially a union of families. Communities do not thrive when families do not function well. Indeed, we are seeing in our country all of the problems—teen pregnancy, juvenile crime, high dropout rates, etc.—created when families break down. Families do not function well when marriages do not last. And marriages cannot last without commitment and trust.

What God forbids in his seventh principle is adultery. But what he is concerned about is marriage. Adultery defined biblically is more than having sex with someone other than your marriage partner (Matthew 5:27, 28). The Bible defines adultery as *anything* that violates a marriage. Therefore, before we look more specifically at adultery, I want us to look more closely at marriage.

2. At the heart of marriage is the permanence of the covenant. God did not make woman just so man could reproduce or release tension. God made the woman because the man was lonely, and God's chief aim for this man–woman design was to let human beings experience togetherness with his or her mate—one mate—for life. From the very beginning, God meant this togetherness to be permanent.

The permanence of the husband–wife relationship is why Genesis 2 tells us that a man should leave his father and mother and be united to his wife. God doesn't say that if the husband and wife decide they're not compatible they can get "un-united."

I'm reminded of the old joke that, when Adam complained he was lonely, God said, "I've got the perfect solution. I'm going to make a woman for you. She's going to be what you always wanted. She's going to love you, support you, honor you! You'll never even have a cross word. She's going to be everything you need."

"That sounds great," Adam replied, "but what is it going to cost me?"

"Well, it'll cost you an arm and a leg," God responded.

And Adam replied, "That's too much. What can I get for a rib?"

The point is this: No one is perfectly compatible with anyone else. The reason that some marriages "work" is not that those two people were lucky enough to find the "right" person for them. It is, instead, that they understand marriage is a covenant intended for a lifetime, and they have invested themselves in making each other's lives happy.

God takes this covenant very seriously, too. Do you remember God's rebuke of the Israelites in

Malachi 2:14? The people do not understand why
God is not accepting their offerings, and God says,
"You ask, 'Why?' It is because the LORD is acting as
the witness between you and the wife of your youth,
because you have broken faith with her, though she
is your partner, the wife of your marriage covenant."

Why does God place such importance on fulfilling
the marriage covenant? It's because staying faithful
to this covenant is an outgrowth of keeping faith
with our covenant to put him first. When Satan
whispers in our ear (and he will), to give it all up, we
remember God's first principle for living: Put God
first! When we make God the Lord of our lives, he
also becomes the Lord of our marriages. His will for
my marriage becomes my priority.

> *When we make God the Lord of our*
> *lives, he also becomes the Lord*
> *of our marriages.*

God's purpose for marriage is togetherness, and
the strength of marriage is in covenanting. Marriages last when both people vow before God to give
themselves fully and permanently to one another in
the face of an unpredictable future. We certainly
don't know what's going to happen tomorrow or what
life holds thirty years from today. But we vow to
each other and to our God that in the midst of all the
unknown in our future, there will be this known:
that we will be together, committed to one another,
whatever may come. We're not basing that promise
on two changeable people but on faith in one unchangeable God—the one who has told us he values
marriage and stands ready to protect it.

Our society, of course, says that kind of commit-

ment is crazy. Today, a marriage is more often
viewed as a contract that clarifies legal positions and
rights but has a limited life expectancy. In fact,
many people have been pragmatic enough to change
the traditional, "outdated" wording of the marriage
vows from "till death do us part" to the more realistic
"for as long as we love each other." After all, there's
no use making commitments we can't (or don't
intend to) keep.

Today, a marriage is more often
viewed as a contract that clarifies
legal positions and rights but has a
limited life expectancy.

It shouldn't surprise us that God's thinking is at
odds with society's, though, should it? What God
says is that, if society is going to work, man must be
related to his wife in marriage like he needs to be
related to God in worship.

3. **At the heart of covenanting is the celebration of intimacy.** The proverb says, "Be faithful to
your own wife and give your love to her alone"
(Proverbs 5:15, TEV). God gave man and woman a
way to consummate and to celebrate this covenant.
A man is going to leave his father and his mother
and be united with his wife. And the two of them
are going to become one flesh.

God talks quite bluntly in the Bible about this
union of bodies. God wants sex to be much more
than just an intimate union of bodies. Because a
covenant is entered by persons, not merely by bodies, sexual relations in marriage should be cel-
ebrated by the whole beings of those involved in the
covenant. Grasping the idea of whole beings coming

together to become one helps us understand why
"casual" sex does such violence to God's will for us.
When two people who can barely recall each other's
name unite, only the bodies are joined.

The sexual aspect of marriage, then, is a God-
designed vehicle for intimate giving, sharing, and
relating with one another that contributes to the
strengthening of the covenant. Certainly, there is
more to a good marriage than good sex. But I have
yet to know of a good marriage without it. God
commands that spouses be responsive to the sexual
needs of their mates. Look at 1 Corinthians 7:2-5a:

> But since there is so much immorality, each
> man should have his own wife, and each
> woman her own husband. The husband should
> fulfill his marital duty to his wife, and likewise
> the wife to her husband. The wife's body does
> not belong to her alone but also to her husband.
> In the same way, the husband's body does not
> belong to him alone but also to his wife. Do not
> deprive each other except by mutual consent
> and for a time, so that you may devote your-
> selves to prayer.

The Bible talks about two kinds of sexual sins, but
the church tends to talk only about one. We've all
heard sermons teaching that it is wrong to give our
bodies to the wrong person, and that is clearly true.
But too often, our churches have been afraid to teach
the rest of God's plan for human sexuality, for the
second sexual sin God condemns is keeping our
bodies from the *right* person.

This God-designed expression of the permanence of
the marriage covenant is so sacred that it is compared to Christ's commitment to his church. In
Ephesians 5:31, 32, we have two of the most amazing

verses in the Bible. Paul says, "For this reason a
man will leave his father and mother and be united
to his wife, and the two will become one flesh. This is
a profound mystery—but I am talking about Christ
and the church." Isn't that incredible? When God
searched the planet for an illustration of how loyal,
faithful, and committed Jesus is to his church, he
thought of the design he made for what happens
when a man and woman covenant together and
celebrate that covenant by becoming one flesh. As
people who wear God's name, we need to understand
that the way we treat our mates is a testimony to an
unbelieving world about God's unbreakable commitment to his people.

It is easy to see, then, why God is displeased when
sex, which he designed, which he made beautiful and
meaningful, is used not to make but to break a
covenant between husband, wife, and himself. Some
people think adultery is wrong because sexual
passion is wrong, but nothing could be farther from
the truth. God made us sexual beings! Some have
said adultery is wrong because reproduction is not
its purpose. Having children is a wonderful thing,
but it's *not* the primary reason God instituted marriage. Some say adultery is wrong because so much
pain is involved, and there certainly is pain. But
even if we could figure out a way to commit adultery
without inflicting pain on anyone, it would still be
wrong because adultery misuses God's symbol of
pledged fidelity. Adultery uses sex to smash rather
than to cement a covenant.

Our culture has separated sex from the oneness of
two people. God treats sex as something holy, but
our culture treats sex lightly. The problem with
treating sex lightly is that it leads to treating people
lightly. In other words, disposable sex makes for
disposable people, and that's a hard way for the

houses of souls to be handled.

Are you beginning to see the faults in the thinking of the people who merely want us to teach our young people how to have "safe" sex? I am for being very careful in our sexual habits, but we sometimes talk about sex as though it were a car or a gun. "When a person's old enough, teach him how to handle it safely, and he'll be okay when he uses it." Let me put this quite bluntly. Sex isn't an object to handle; it is something sacred designed by God for a purpose. When we use it outside that purpose, even if we use it safely, we use it wrongly. And somebody *will* get hurt.

A Look at Adultery

What does it mean, then, to break the marriage covenant through adultery? Three very clear teachings of Scripture deal with what it means to break the covenant.

1. Physical Adultery

The most obvious way to break the covenant is through physical adultery—through participating in sexual intercourse with a person who is not your marriage partner. Why would anyone want a sexual encounter outside the context of a covenant? It could be because that person would rather receive than give. God designed sex in marriage to be a giving act. Sex out of marriage is a taking act. And it does great violence to marriage. It *uses* human beings, which is detestable in the eyes of the Lord. Hebrews 13:4 makes God's point: "Marriage should be honored by all and the marriage bed kept pure, for God will judge the adulterer and all the sexually immoral." We can violate our covenant through physical adultery.

2. Mental Adultery

God wants us to understand that, as with every other aspect of our lives, the way we handle our sexuality is primarily a matter of *inner* purity. We don't have to physically betray our covenant to break faith with our mate; we can also violate our covenant through fantasizing about and dwelling on the possibility of sex with someone other than our marriage partner. Jesus said, "You have heard that it was said, 'Do not commit adultery.' But I tell you that anyone who looks at a woman lustfully has already committed adultery with her in his heart" (Matthew 5:27, 28).

When I was a teenager, I thought lust was thinking about having sex with somebody and being willing to do it, but refraining because you don't think you can "get away with it." But that definition lets us off the hook. It would be very hard to convince me, after all the couples I've seen in counseling, that God is pleased when we sit around for extended periods of time and sexually fantasize about someone who is not our marriage partner, even if we never intend to act on those fantasies. The thought of covenant-breaking cannot improve togetherness and intimacy in our marriages. Jesus says lust is a covenant-breaker.

3. Legalistic Adultery

This is the kind of adultery in which someone wants to break his or her marriage covenant, but for some reason—fear of career repercussions or loss of social standing (perhaps even within the social structure of a church)—the person wants to make breaking the covenant look legitimate. So they divorce their first mate in order to marry the person with whom they are "more compatible."

Trying to beat the system, so to speak, is not a
new trick, of course. People have been trying for a
long, long time to appear to comply with God's laws
while still doing whatever they want. In fact, people
were playing this exact game in Jesus' day. The
Jews knew God's teaching on the permanence of
marriage, but they wanted a way around his law. So,
whenever a Jew saw a woman who pleased him
more than his current wife, he went home, handed
the wife a piece of paper announcing their divorce,
and started preparing for the next wedding.

Jesus, however, saw through the proper legal
forms these religious people used and condemned
them for their motives: "Anyone who divorces his
wife and marries another woman commits adultery
against her. And if she divorces her husband and
marries another man, she commits adultery" (Mark
10:11, 12). In other words, Jesus says, "Whom do you
think you are fooling? Don't you think God sees
through your actions and knows what's in your
heart?" Treating a spouse this way may be legal, but
God says it isn't moral.

These people remind me of a story I heard once
about W. C. Fields, no friend of the Christian faith.
One day a friend of Fields entered his dressing room
and was amazed to find the old comedian reading
the Bible. When the friend asked Fields what he was
doing, he shut the Book and, looking rather embarrassed, replied, "Looking for loopholes, just looking
for loopholes."

Now, I'm not saying, and Jesus did not say, that
everyone who has been divorced is an adulterer.
Many people experience what they never intended or
sought—the pain of divorce. The church has much to
learn about receiving these hurting folks and helping them experience acceptance and healing. But
Jesus did teach that God is not fooled by those who

break covenant with their mates in their hearts and then use the courts to make their hard-heartedness look aboveboard. People of character want to be moral, not just legal.

---

*People of character want to be
moral, not just legal.*

The court of the land does not care why you want to break your contract. But the Judge of the universe does care why we break our covenants, and, what's more, he knows when we do. He is, after all, the God who searches hearts, and, ultimately, all adultery is a problem of the heart. Because very few of us have hearts that aren't a bit adulterated, very few of us have a right to throw any stones. What we do have is a need for a strategy—a way to behave as people of character in a sex-saturated world.

The Need for a Strategy

Don't Flirt with Impurity

There are some ventures in which the objective is to see how close to danger a person can go and still survive. You may remember how in the movie *The Right Stuff*, for example, the test pilots were constantly "pushing the envelope" to see how fast, how high they could push themselves and their machines. And the men who had the nerve to cross barriers others thought uncrossable and who lived to tell about the experience were thought to have the "right stuff."

But seeing how far we can push ourselves without crashing and burning is not the "right stuff" for marriage. For a married person, the term "innocent

flirtation" is a contradiction. People of character
must be very conscious of what they listen to, what
they watch, what they say, what they do, and with
whom they associate, so that no one would question
their commitment to purity. See what Jesus said
after his teaching on lusting:

> "If your right eye causes you to sin, gouge it out
> and throw it away. It is better for you to lose
> one part of your body than for your whole body
> to be thrown into hell. And if your right hand
> causes you to sin, cut it off and throw it away.
> It is better for you to lose one part of your body
> than for your whole body to go into hell"
> (Matthew 5:29, 30).

The story of Joseph and Potiphar's wife is recorded in Genesis 39. Joseph worked for Potiphar,
and Potiphar's wife was infatuated with her
husband's servant. Finally, one day when she and
Joseph were alone in the house, she tried to seduce
him, but, instead of just saying no and going about
his business in the house or staying around and
lecturing her on morality, Joseph ran away. He
didn't wait to see how long he could stay around this
woman before he crossed the line. He got away! This
is exactly the advice Paul gives when he says,

> Flee from sexual immorality. All other sins a
> man commits are outside his body, but he who
> sins sexually sins against his own body. Do you
> not know that your body is a temple of the Holy
> Spirit, who is in you, whom you have received
> from God? You are not your own; you were
> bought at a price. Therefore honor God with
> your body (1 Corinthians 6:18).

In other words, if you are tempted to have sex outside of God's design, get away before you dishonor the Holy Spirit's temple!

A young preacher was visiting one day with an older preacher. The older man was advising the younger one to be especially careful in guarding against sexual sin, and the young preacher assured his mentor, "Oh, I'm always careful. I always hang out with a big group of people. You know what they say: 'There's safety in numbers!' "

"Yes, son," the old preacher replied, "but there's more safety in exodus."

People of character don't flirt with impurity.

Enrich Your Marriage

Our mates should not get our time, our energy, or our bodies after everyone else. Our marriage covenants are supposed to be earthly illustrations of God's faithfulness to his people, so we need to make our marriages a priority.

There's a big difference between cherishing and not cheating.

You may be saying, "Well, I don't cheat on my mate." But God is also concerned about whether you cherish your mate. God never calls us to do the minimum possible to follow his teachings. God says in the seventh principle that he does *not* want us to commit adultery. But on a deeper level it teaches that God *does* want us to do the kinds of things that enhance and celebrate our covenant and that communicate that we hold it and our partner precious.

There's a big difference between cherishing and

not cheating. I wonder what it was like for Adam and Eve. When she asked Adam if he still loved her, did he say sourly, "Who else would I love?" or did he take her in his arms, look into her eyes, and say, "Eve, you're the only girl in the world for me!"

I have a seventy-year-old friend who loved her husband so much you could just see it in her face. She looked at him with the most adoring eyes, as though she was looking right into his soul. You could tell, she thought he was the most intelligent, witty, handsome man on earth. Even during his last days, thin and frail and suffering from cancer, she continued to see him as the "hunk" she knew as a young man. That's cherishing your mate!

Your marriage might be in the doldrums right now. It might be in a rut, and it might take a lot of work to rekindle that fire and make it burn again. But the price you pay to rekindle your marriage is far, far smaller than the price you pay for adultery. So make your marriage a priority. People of character work to enrich their marriage.

Purity Is a Choice

In writing this chapter, I am concerned about those who think they don't need this lesson. Many counseling sessions begin with "I never thought I could do such a thing." In the sea of sexual sin, pride almost always goes before the fall (Proverbs 16:18). I'm also concerned about those who think it's come too late because they've already blown it. Look at God's encouraging words:

> Do you not know that the wicked will not inherit the kingdom of God? Do not be deceived: Neither the sexually immoral nor idolaters nor adulterers nor male prostitutes

nor homosexual offenders nor thieves nor the
greedy nor drunkards nor slanderers nor
swindlers will inherit the kingdom of God. And
that is what some of you were. But you were
washed, you were sanctified, you were justified
in the name of the Lord Jesus Christ and by
the Spirit of our God (1 Corinthians 6:9-11).

Church is the best place in the world for adulter-
ers to be. It always has been. If you're guilty of
adultery, you can sit right down with the swindlers
and the liars and all the rest of us sinners who
desperately need the blood of Jesus so we can stand
justified before God. People of character admit their
need for strength and cleansing. We don't need to
throw stones at people. We just need to admit how
much each of us needs God's Spirit to live holy lives,
for we are all fallen, sinful creatures. All of us have
things in our hearts that adulterate our worship to
God. All of us at one time or another have needed to
hear Jesus say to us, "Neither do I condemn you. Go
your way and sin no more."

On a summer Sunday morning in 1974 in
Pittsburg, Pennsylvania, the minister concluded a
powerful sermon on the virtues of living a life of
sexual purity. The song leader began singing "Just
as I Am," and a woman who was visiting for the first
time came down the aisle and sat down on the front
pew.

When the song ended, the minister announced to
the congregation that this woman, named Wanda,
had something she wanted to say to the church.

Wanda walked to the microphone, dry-eyed and
smiling. "Good morning. My name is Wanda. And
I'm a prostitute."

You could hear all the longtime members suck air

in shock at her unprecedented statement. And dead
silence fell over the room.

Wanda continued, "I want to study the Bible and
find out what's wrong with my life because I know
that something is definitely wrong. I just don't know
for sure what it is. Your minister today has shown
me part of my problem, and I'm thankful for that. I
want to know what else is wrong. I hope you will be
kind enough to let me visit your meetings until I can
study through the Bible and learn how to be different. I want to be pure like you." And she sat down.

Over the next few weeks, dynamic changes began
to take place—not just in Wanda, but in that whole
congregation. Others began to come before the
church to admit their impurities in different areas of
their lives. Love flowed as brothers and sisters
confessed their sins to each other. And God's Word
led many of them to purer lives in his service.

Wanda changed. She gave up prostitution, went to
work in a local hospital as a nurse's assistant, and
learned to help people in pain. She received several
promotions for her outstanding work and developed
into a happy, joyful person. Purity had replaced
prostitution; God had replaced godlessness. Wanda
became a person of character.

Sexual impurity is not the unforgivable sin.
Through the ages, people like Wanda have successfully turned away from their immorality and have
been forgiven by God. That's what the grace of God
and forgiveness are all about. He can and will forgive you, too.

Focusing Your Faith

1. What's the biggest lie that Satan tries to sell you regarding sex.

2. W. C. Fields said he was "looking for loopholes" in the Bible. What do you hear people say today that tells you they are looking for loopholes in God's teaching about sex?

3. The Bible defines adultery as *anything* that violates a marriage. How else can you violate your marriage besides sexually?

4. Why do we think "it would never happen to me" when it comes to adultery?

5. How would you help a struggling friend with an unfaithful mate? A friend who is unfaithful?

6. "Disposable sex makes for disposable people." How does it feel to be *used* and then discarded? How can that happen even within a marriage?

7. Should you as a Christian get involved in political issues such as abortion, AIDS, and homosexuality? Should the church?

Chapter 10

Terms of Surrender

᭍

Mahmoud, the
first Mohammedan
conqueror of India, was
about to die. Did he
call for his god, his
priest, or his family?
No. He ordered all his
costly apparel, his
vessels of silver and
gold, and his pearls and precious stones to be dis-
played around him. In the extravagant royal resi-
dence at Ghuznee, which Mahmoud called the
Palace of Felicity, he touched the display and wept
like a child.

"What toils," said Mahmoud, "what dangers, what
fatigues, both of body and mind, have I endured for
the sake of acquiring these treasures, and what
cares in preserving them! And now I am about to
die and leave them."

Principle 8:

*Keep "Things" in
Perspective*

*Exodus 20:15
Ephesians 4:28*

That's what happens when people place their faith in "things" rather than in God. They are disappointed at the end. And the end always comes. Here's another example.

One day a fairy came to a man and told him she would grant him any favor he might wish. The man thought about it for a few minutes, and then he said, "My wish is to see a newspaper published one year from today."

Immediately, the fairy handed him a newspaper printed one year in advance. He turned quickly to the financial page, ran his fingers nervously up and down the list of stocks, and leaping from his chair he shouted, "Hurrah! I'm worth 15 million dollars!"

Then he casually turned over to the obituary page, where his glance fell on a report that made him gasp. "I died two days ago!"

Have you ever had anything stolen from you? When Jamie and I were first married, our home was robbed. It happened one Sunday morning while we were at church. They took all of Jamie's jewelry, quite a few of our wedding gifts, and, worst of all, our television set! To make matters worse, it was the first day of football season, and those thieves kept me from seeing the Dallas Cowboys' opening game! Needless to say, God taught us a valuable lesson early in our marriage: you can't build your life around "things" because you can't count on "things" to always be there. (But I still think there must be a special punishment for someone who'd steal your TV on the Cowboys' opening day!)

In a sense, the first sin of eating the forbidden fruit in the Garden of Eden was a theft, for the man and the woman took what God had told them to leave alone. And the very first sin recorded after the children of Israel came into the promised land was a theft. Achan stole the riches of Canaan after God had forbidden it. His sin caused him to lose not just his inheritance of the promised land, but all that he had, including his family and his own life (Joshua 7).

It doesn't matter how much or how little you take, stealing is wrong. You can't be a person of character and be a thief.

My first vivid memory of a sin was a theft. I don't remember how old I was, but I remember my brother and I took sack lunches to school every day, and every day our mother left us each seven cents to buy a carton of milk to drink with our lunch. One morning, though, two cartons of milk sounded good to me, so I took my seven cents and Mark's, too. Now, stealing seven cents may not sound like much to you, but I learned something that day. It doesn't matter how much or how little you take, stealing is wrong. You can't be a person of character and be a thief.

We all have something inside of us that is fascinated with the concept of getting something for nothing. It permeates our culture. It even invades the church. You would probably be shocked to know how many times a month thieves come into our church building and steal things. They steal video equipment. They steal stereo and sound equipment. They even steal Bibles!

Two of our Sunday school teachers recently told me that thieves were coming into their classroom during the week and stealing money the five year olds were saving to give to our missionaries. The teachers would lock up the money every week, but the thieves would do whatever they had to do, even tear doors off hinges, to get the coins these children had brought to church.

Finally, when the lead teacher had had enough, he wrote a note to the thief and placed it in the can of money. Sure enough, the next Sunday when the teacher arrived, he saw the hinges had been forced open again. But when he checked the can, it still rattled. He reread the note inside: "Dear thief, Our class has been saving and collecting money to buy Bibles and food for poor children. Please don't take it anymore. God loves you, The kindergarten class."

Then scrawled at the bottom in a different hand was, "Dear class, I'm sorry I took your money. I won't take it anymore. The thief."

Stealing is a part of the American culture, and, unfortunately, it's invading the church. But God's instruction for people who seek his character is quite clear: *You shall not steal* (Exodus 20:15). I have learned, however, that dealing with stealing is no easy matter. And it goes much deeper than the pickpocket who steals a purse so he can buy some cheap wine. When God says, "Don't steal," he's also talking about the kind of dishonesty that lives in your heart and mine.

Two Ways to Own

Why do people steal? Perhaps some people steal for self-preservation. They are so destitute that they think stealing is the only way they can survive. Many today steal because they have expensive drug habits that their legitimate jobs simply can't support. For some it's an illness. And some apparently steal for excitement. It's not that they don't have things, but they want the thrill of getting away with doing something wrong.

I don't think that's why most people steal, though. Most people steal because they have not kept material things in perspective. We live in times dominated by a materialistic worldview where ownership of things has become a measure of affirmation and self-worth. Why in the world do people buy $150,000 cars? Will that car get them someplace better or faster than a $20,000 car? No, but if Joe drives an expensive car, his neighbors look at him and say, "Wow, he can afford a $150,000 car!" And that makes Joe feel more important.

You Own Things

Before we go any further, we need to acknowledge that, in giving his eighth principle, God implies a right to own property. In other words, there is a wrong of taking because there is a right of keeping. From the beginning God created people to be care-takers. When we have nothing to show for our work, when we have nothing to use and nothing to care for, we are diminished in spirit. It is okay for us to own things.

---

*There is a wrong of taking
because there is a right of keeping.*

Still, we must be very careful in upholding a right to ownership, because God never gives the Haves the right to oppress the Have Nots. Scripture, contrary to communism, does not condemn private ownership. But Scripture, contrary to capitalism, does not go to the other extreme and assert an absolute right to private ownership.

God has never condoned the accumulation of wealth at the cost of others' well-being. This divine compassion for those without the economic advan-tage was behind the laws establishing the year of

Jubilee (Leviticus 25). Jubilee was the year which came every seven sabbaths of years (forty-nine years) in which all debts were to be cancelled, and all the land that had been sold was to be returned to the family that had originally owned it. In other words, every forty-nine years, God wanted the wealth of the land redistributed, so that the rich could not just keep accumulating more and more wealth at the expense of the poor. As the Lord explains it in verse 23, "The land must not be sold permanently, because the land is mine and you are but aliens and my tenants."

Scripture teaches that all a person has comes from God and is a trust. Perhaps then, we should think in terms of stewardship instead of ownership, for, while ownership of things is not a transgression, it certainly is a test. People of character may own things, but they don't accumulate things at the expense of other people, because they know that God made things to be used and people to be loved.

Things Own You

We live in times when "things" define our personal value, and, if we buy into this materialistic value system, we will inevitably want more and more things. Eventually we will reach the point that we are tested morally as to what we will do in order to get more "things." Scripture, on the other hand, urges us to keep "things" in a proper perspective. These verses illustrate:

> "What good will it be for a man if he gains the whole world, yet forfeits his soul?" (Matthew 16:26).

> "Be on your guard against all kinds of greed; a man's life does not consist in the abundance of

his possessions" (Luke 12:15).

For we brought nothing into this world, and we
can take nothing out of it. But if we have food
and clothing, we will be content with that
(1 Timothy 6:7, 8).

We must live with a delicate balance. It's all right
to own things, but that right does not justify grabbing for everything we can get. The thief's root
problem is his dissatisfaction with the portion God
has allotted him in life. As the preacher in
Ecclesiastes 5:10 says, "Whoever loves money never
has money enough; whoever loves wealth is never
satisfied with his income."

A classic example of this connection between
dissatisfaction and theft is recorded in 1 Kings 21. In
this passage, King Ahab, the richest man in Israel,
is upset because a poor man named Naboth won't
sell his garden. Ahab is frustrated. He cannot rest or
sleep; he can only sulk because he believes he needs
this one additional thing to make him happy, and he
can't get it. His desire for this property so over-
whelms him that his wife, Jezebel, plots and orders
Naboth's murder in order to get the land. For their
wickedness, God condemned this couple. Speaking
for the LORD, Elijah said,

> "I have found you . . . because you have sold
> yourself to do evil in the eyes of the LORD. 'I am
> going to bring disaster on you. I will consume
> your descendants and cut off from Ahab every
> last male in Israel—slave or free. . . .' And also
> concerning Jezebel the LORD says: 'Dogs will
> devour Jezebel by the wall of Jezreel' " (verses
> 20b, 21, 23).

Their character crisis had disastrous consequences.

The thief takes because he's not content with what he has. It's not a question of physical need but of spiritual deficiency. He sees the things the LORD has given him, shakes his fist at the Almighty, and says, "This is not enough. I deserve more, and if you will not provide it for me, then I'll just take it myself." His real struggle is spiritual in nature. That's why I think any genuine rehabilitation of a thief must deal with his spiritual nature. A thief can learn a skill, and he can get a job, but until he learns to be content with what God has given him, he will always be tempted to take what God has given others.

Two Ways to Steal

People of character keep "things" in perspective. Those who don't, concoct countless ways to rob their fellow man and even rob God.

Robbing Your Neighbor

We can rob our neighbor, first, by taking what he should have. It's easy to rationalize taking things, isn't it? "After all, they can afford it." "He's got so much, and I've got so little." "No harm was done." "They'll never miss it." But no matter how we try to justify our actions, God never gives us any reason to think he approves of our taking what he has given to another. The fundamental principle of biblical ethics is still, "In everything, do to others what you would have them do to you . . ." (Matthew 7:12).

Do you take what belongs to others? Don't be too quick to say no. There are all sorts of ways we can take what others should have. Obviously, we can take their property, like the thieves did at our house on that Sunday morning. But there are other ways to steal, as well.

Do you steal ideas? And then do you take credit for them as though they were your own? Probably in much of today's business world, stolen information is much more costly than stolen equipment. Plagiarism is a kind of stealing that can be especially tempting. Preachers, I've found, often struggle with the temptation to plagiarize. We get tapes and read books as resources for our sermons, which is great, but we sometimes cross a line where we begin taking credit for work which is not our own.

I heard a tape one time of a minister who was preaching one of my sermons. Not only was he using my sermon, but he told a story out of my life as though it had happened to him! I think that day he crossed the line.

One way some churches today steal ideas that belong to others is by illegal photocopying. In other words, we *keep* the price of the products we copy for ourselves, rather than giving it to the author or publisher to whom it rightfully belongs. For instance, do your teachers make copies of student handouts and activity pages, rather than buying a student book for each student? Does your chorus or singing group make photocopies of music, rather than buying a sheet of music for each singer? Sometimes this is done out of ignorance of copyright laws. Sometimes it's excused by "I'm only copying a little," or "I'm only doing it to save the church money." What most of us don't realize, though, is that when we don't pay for the information we use, we're hurting ourselves.

Do you steal money by not paying your debts? The Bible says when a debt is due, we should pay it. Of course, we can devise all kinds of ways to get out of paying what we owe, and we can even get out of it legally through bankruptcy. But people of character live by a higher standard than the loopholes in the laws of the land.

I'm not saying we never make financial mistakes. The congregation where I preach, for example, built a new building in the late 1980s when the Texas economy was as bright as it's ever been. A few years into making payments on the building, however, the economy fell apart. Some of our church members lost their jobs and had to move away. Others lost their businesses and financial bases and, so, were not able financially to give what they had pledged to pay for the building. And the land our leaders had expected to sell to repay the debt lost half its value. That left us holding the bag, and the bag was empty!

Legally, we could have declared bankruptcy as a church, let our creditors foreclose on the building, and probably could have bought it back for thirty to fifty cents on the dollar. But we believed that while that action might have been legal, according to the Texas code, it would not have been ethical, according to God's code.

We prayed for God to provide a way that we could resolve this situation without dishonoring him, and he allowed us to renegotiate the church debt so that we would eventually pay back everything we owe— all the principal and all the interest.

That was a humbling experience I never want to go through again. If you are struggling with over-whelming debt right now, my heart goes out to you. But let me encourage you to pray that God will show you a way to deal with your creditors in as fair a way as possible. He is faithful.

Do you steal money through swindling? One of the most frequent forms of stealing in our culture is swindling. I am concerned for those of you in the business world that business pressures will blur your line between dealing and stealing. Too often once we start the gamesmanship of negotiations, winning the game rather than protecting our integrity becomes paramount. A lot of deals are done by taking advantage of somebody else's distress, ignorance, or weakness, and we defend our strategy by claiming it's just "good business." I'd like to disagree. It's business, but I don't think it's good.

This temptation isn't limited to big business. Have you ever sold a used car? When a potential buyer comes and asks if the car has any problems, how honest are you? Leaving out a few pertinent details may be "part of the game," but my question is, "Is this a game we should be playing?"

"But everyone does it," you may argue. "It's industry standard." And it might very well be. But even if everyone else is "doing it," majority opinion has never been the deciding point for people of character. *You* have to make the decisions about how you conduct your business affairs. Remember that people of character have chosen to adopt God's, not industry's, standards. In 1 Corinthians 6, Paul says God has excluded both thieves and swindlers from his kingdom.

Do you steal time? Do you take checks for forty hours' work when you only gave thirty-seven? Or do you steal by not paying your employees fairly, by not giving them what they've earned through hard work? Perhaps you steal others' time by being consistently late to appointments or meetings.

Do you steal opportunity through discrimination? Do you refuse people a chance because of skin color or sex? If you do, you've stolen something from them.

Do you steal liberty? You can steal liberty in the church through binding traditions on people where God meant there to be freedom. That kind of stealing is called legalism. It's a theft of the grace of God.

Do you steal well-being? We can rob our neighbor

by *taking* what he should have, but we can also rob
our neighbor by *keeping* what he should have. We
have said that taking is wrong, but does the fact that
taking is wrong mean keeping is always right? Let
me ask you this: Is it morally right for us to accumulate more things than we can use in a lifetime when
others have nothing?

> *Is it morally right for us to
> accumulate more things than we
> can use in a lifetime when others
> have nothing?*

We talked earlier about God's attitude toward
those who make their fortune by stepping on the
backs of the poor, but God also holds us accountable
for the good we do with "well-gotten" gain. In Luke
16 we have Jesus' parable of the rich man and
Lazarus. When the rich man died, he went to hell.
Jesus tells us nothing of the man's attendance at
synagogue or any of his religious convictions. He
says nothing to condemn the means by which the
man gathered his fortune either. All he really tells
us of him is that every day as the rich man left his
house he passed the beggar Lazarus, and he did
nothing to rescue Lazarus from his state of despair.
The rich man failed to follow God's instruction
because he kept what the beggar should have been
given. Perhaps the moral right to property is more
difficult to determine than the legal one.

Robbing God

"Things" can own any of us, whether we are rich
or poor. And giving our hearts to "things" means
taking our hearts from God. For when accumulating

material possessions becomes so important that our attitudes and actions are driven by our desire to accumulate, we've given "things" first place instead of God. We rob God for the same reason we rob our neighbors: we've lost our perspective on "things." We can rob God in several ways.

We rob God of credibility by living lives lacking in character. God spoke through Jeremiah to the people,

> " 'Will you steal and murder, commit adultery and perjury, burn incense to Baal and follow other gods you have not known, and then come and stand before me in this house, which bears my Name, and say, "We are safe"— safe to do all these detestable things? Has this house, which bears my Name, become a den of robbers to you?' " (Jeremiah 7:9-11).

When we ignore God's instructions for living while wearing his name, we don't just destroy community, we defame him. When we ignore God's absolute values for living, when we murder and steal, when we commit adultery and lie, when we go about our business cheating and swindling others and then show up at church as though we represent his plan for people, we rob him of the glory due his name. We ought to live to give God glory, but we can live so that glory is taken away. We rob God by ignoring his Code of Ethics.

We rob God of honor by giving him meager offerings. Malachi quotes God as saying,

> Will a man rob God? Yet you rob me. But you ask, "How do we rob you?"
>
> "In tithes and offerings. You are under a

curse—the whole nation of you—because you
are robbing me. Bring the whole tithe into the
storehouse, that there may be food in my
house. Test me in this, . . . and see if I will not
throw open the floodgates of heaven and pour
out so much blessing that you will not have
room enough for it" (Malachi 3:8-10).

The Lord is greatly dishonored and displeased by
meager offerings. Such paltry giving reveals two
problems with our hearts. First, it shows that our
hearts don't care for the hurting and lost the way
God's does. And, second, stinginess toward God
reveals a faith problem, because we trust our possessions, not God, to provide for our needs.

I'm a great believer in tithing. I've heard people
claim that tithing was merely part of the Old Testament, so Christians are not bound by that concept.
But in all my studies of God's Word, I have yet to
find an instance when Christ called his followers to a
lower standard than Moses did. In fact, rather than
going below the law, grace always calls us beyond
the law.

------

*Rather than going below the law,
grace always calls us
beyond the law.*

There's a big difference between giving under law
and giving under grace. Some of you may have
worked in situations where your employer pressured
you to give money to one charity or another, regardless of whether you felt like supporting that charity's
work. When it came time to put down your payroll
deduction amount, how much did you give? I'll bet

it was the least amount you could get away with, wasn't it? That's giving under law.

When Christmas rolls around, though, Jamie and I don't sit down and discuss what is the least amount we can spend on our children and still look like respectable parents. We go to the toy store, and we want to buy every item we see that would be good for the kids! In fact, we have to restrain ourselves so that we don't spend more than we can afford (and more than would be good for the kids)! Because we love those kids so much, our thinking is not how much *must* we give; it's how much *can* we give. That's giving under grace.

If you don't see any way in your financial situation that you can tithe right now, let me challenge you to pray for guidance, then set for yourself a course of action, so that in two, three, or four years, you will be able to give God an offering that honors him. Just, please, don't rob God. Some of the most hardened thieves in the world pack pews every Sunday. But God says that willingness to sacrifice things to honor him and to help men is a true mark of a person of character.

Three Ways to Surrender

There are three ways to guard our hearts against the temptation to steal. They involve surrendering all to God. You could call them God's Terms of Surrender.

1. Cultivate a Thankful Spirit

Thanksgiving is not a holiday for God's child; it's a lifestyle. I've always appreciated a story about Matthew Henry, author of a great commentary on the Bible. It seems the old English scholar was robbed one day as he was walking down the street.

In his diary that day, he made the following entry:

> Let me be thankful, first, because I was never
> robbed before. Second, because, although they
> took my wallet, they did not take my life.
> Third, because, although they took my all, it
> was not much. And, fourth, because it was I
> who was robbed, and not I who robbed.

People of character remember how much God has
given them and how much more that is than they
deserve.

2. Share Whenever You Can

Many early Christians were former thieves. A lot
of others lost their jobs or businesses as a result of
becoming Christians and, so, faced the temptation to
steal. But Paul advises them, "He who has been
stealing must steal no longer, but must work, doing
something useful with his own hands, that he may
have something to share with those in need"
(Ephesians 4:28). Sharing is an indispensable part of
owning things to the glory of God. Did you know
there are more promises in the Bible related to your
sharing than to anything else? One is: "A generous
man will prosper; he who refreshes others will
himself be refreshed" (Proverbs 11:25).

The story is told that the great English preacher,
Charles Spurgeon, was invited by a wealthy English-
man to speak at the country church where the
wealthy man worshiped. It seems the congregation
was trying to pay off some debt and they thought
having a famous preacher speak that day might help
the contribution. So the wealthy member wrote
Spurgeon, inviting him to speak and offering to let
him stay in his townhouse, his country home, or his
cottage by the sea. Spurgeon, it is said, wrote back a

terse note saying, "I'm not coming. Sell one of your places, and take care of the debt yourself."

The point is that becoming a Christian gives us a new worldview, an entirely different perspective with regard to things. In our old value system, things were to be acquired at all costs. In God's value system, however, they are merely to be acquired so we can use them to meet people's needs. People of character want to share whenever they can.

3. Trust God

Have you noticed how each principle has a way of coming back to the first? If God is not Lord *of* all, he is not Lord *at* all. That's why and how people of character keep "things" in perspective. Trusting God is the only way we can keep our proper perspective on things. Jesus knew about thieves, and he knew about how things can own our lives. That's why he spoke so strongly about the foolishness of spending our lives trying to store up what we cannot keep:

> "Do not store up for yourselves treasures on earth, where moth and rust destroy, and where thieves break in and steal. But store up for yourselves treasures in heaven, where moth and rust do not destroy, and where thieves do not break in and steal. For where your treasure is, there your heart will be also" (Matthew 6:19-21).

Instead of putting our trust in "things," Jesus advises, "Seek first his kingdom and his righteousness, and all these things will be given to you as well " (Matthew 6:33). Trust God. Put God first. It's as simple as that.

Focusing Your Faith

1. "God made things to be used and people to be loved." Describe two or three ways that we may often reverse this idea.

2. Ecclesiastes 5:10 says, "Whoever loves money never has money enough. . . ." Go to a mirror, look yourself in the eye, and ask yourself how this scripture applies to you personally.

3. What lesson has God taught you recently to help you keep "things" in perspective?

4. In regard to giving, "Grace always calls us beyond the law." If you truly believe this truth in your own heart, how will your giving be affected?

5. We're dependent on "things" now more than ever before. What necessities do you own now that 20 years ago would have been considered luxuries?

6. Have you ever been angry at God for taking someone or something away from you? What did you learn from that experience?

7. Consider the Jewish year of Jubilee. How would you feel about having to return your land to the original owner? How would you feel if you owed a debt that would be forgiven?

Chapter 11

The Great
American Lie

಄

W hen he was
twenty-four years old,
Abraham Lincoln
served as the postmas-
ter of New Salem,
Illinois, for which he
was paid an annual
salary of $55.70.

Principle 9:

Tell the Truth

Exodus 20:16
Colossians 3:9, 10

The New Salem post
office was closed in 1836, but it was several years
before an agent arrived from Washington to settle
accounts with ex-postmaster Lincoln, who was a
struggling lawyer not doing too well.

The agent informed him that there was seventeen
dollars due the government. Lincoln crossed the
room, opened an old trunk and took out a yellowed
cotton rag bound with string.

Untying it, he spread out the cloth and there was
the seventeen dollars. He had been holding it for all

those years. "I never use any man's money but my own," he said. Lincoln could have lied to the agent about the money and would have probably gotten away with it. But even then, twenty-four years before he entered the White House, the rail splitter was showing the character that earned him the title of "Honest Abe."

Don't you wish our government officials and American citizens were as truthful and honest today as Honest Abe?

The truth is, we are living the Great American Lie. Truth has become a rarity, a joke, a has-been virtue that few have and even fewer want.

Some lies in America have been used so often they are joked about. Doug Mushrow has written an article titled "19 Great American Lies." Here are twelve of his classics:

1. The check is in the mail.
2. I'll start my diet tomorrow.
3. We service what we sell.
4. Give me your number, and the doctor will call you right back.
5. Money cheerfully refunded.
6. One size fits all.
7. This hurts me more than it hurts you.
8. I just need 5 minutes of your time.
9. Your table will be ready in a few minutes.
10. Let's have lunch sometime.
11. It's not the money; it's the principle.
12. I'm from the federal government, and I'm here to help you.

Lying is an accepted way of life for many of us, but we forget that lying can sometimes get us into trouble. Take, for instance, the four students who got spring fever and decided to skip their morning classes. They showed up after lunch, apologized to their teacher, and said they were late because they'd had a flat. "Take your seats," the teacher responded. "You missed a pop quiz, so get out a piece of paper. First question, 'Which tire was it?'"

Even though we joke about the subject, deep down most of us don't think lying is really all that funny. We can pay a heavy price for not living with the truth. Just ask Gary Hart. As a would-be Democratic presidential candidate in 1988, Hart was plagued by rumors of womanizing. He stood before the press and denied all the accusations, daring the reporters to follow him and see if he was not speaking the truth. Unfortunately for Mr. Hart, the press took him up on the challenge, and his extra-marital affair was no longer merely a rumor; it was a proven fact, and his quest for the presidency ended in shame.

God doesn't think lying is funny, either. Lying destroys relationships, and it perverts justice. Lying destroys trust and fractures families. And, for people who claim to follow God, telling lies misrepresents the One whose basic nature is truth. Proverbs 6:16-19 teaches:

> There are six things the LORD hates,
> seven that are detestable to him:
> haughty eyes,
> a lying tongue,
> hands that shed innocent blood,
> a heart that devises wicked schemes,
> feet that are quick to rush into evil,
> a false witness who pours out lies
> and a man who stirs up dissension among
>   brothers.

We desperately need to return to the clear call of God to tell the truth. That's the ninth of God's instructions for being people of character. It's found in Exodus 20:16, and it reads like this: *You shall not give false testimony against your neighbor.* Now, the specific application in the instruction refers to speaking the truth in legal matters. Of course, prohibiting perjury is essential, for no community can hope to maintain any standard of justice for its people if its courts cannot determine the truth.

But the undergirding principle of the ninth instruction is that in all areas of our lives God demands honesty. Simply reading the first three chapters of Genesis shows us that Satan's lies plunged this world into a terrible mess. And reading the Gospels makes it quite clear that false accusations sent Jesus to the cross. God never intended his people to be involved with deceit and dishonesty. In our words, just like in every other aspect of our lives, God wants his people of character to model themselves after him. And God Almighty never lies.

As Frederick William Robertson observed, "Truth lies in character. Christ did not simply speak the truth; he was Truth—Truth through and through, for truth is a thing not of words but a life and being."

As disciples of Christ, we must not only *speak* the truth in words; we must *be* truth through and through. Truth must permeate our entire life and being.

What's a Lie?

A lie is an intentional deception. Sometimes people choose to completely abandon reality in what they say. In my home state of Texas, we have recently seen the downfall of one of our political rising stars, because her opponent discovered that what she had told the world about her academic accomplishments was absolutely false. She was on record as saying she had graduated with honors from a state university, when, in fact, she had not graduated at all. And while she was in school, she was only a mediocre student. She intentionally presented false data about herself to the public she was supposed to serve.

To Err Without Lying

Sometimes we lie and err, but it is possible to err without lying. In other words, I might tell you that the Cowboy game starts at 3:00 P.M. Sunday, believing that to be true, when, in actuality, the kick-off is at 12:00. That's not a lie; it's a mistake. My children like to give their explanations of things, like how electricity works or how an airplane flies, and what they say is not accurate, but they are not lying because they believe what they are saying is true.

To Lie Without Erring

We can also lie without erring. We can tell the truth in a manner that people are deceived. As the 1992 Democratic presidential candidate, Bill Clinton faced a storm of criticism over this type of deception. Asked time and again if he had ever smoked marijuana, Clinton's patent reply was, "I have never broken the laws of this country." But, when he was finally pinned down on the question, he admitted that while he was in England as a student he had used the drug. All those other times he'd been asked the question, he was not giving erroneous information, for U.S. law lacks the jurisdiction to prohibit smoking marijuana in another country. But, while he was not erring, he was also not telling the truth—a fact he finally admitted.

Why Lie?

We seem to have a love/hate relationship with lying. Indeed, deception is built into the very fabric of our culture. Jamie and I are teaching our children to think about what commercials say and laugh at the claims they make, whether specifically expressed (Can Treasure Trolls really grant little girls' wishes?) or implied (If we drink the right kind of beer, will we really be beautiful, athletic, and popular with the opposite sex?).

But dishonesty is built into other areas of society as well. It's understandable that the state politician who was discredited was tempted to lie on her résumé. Résumé "padding" (doesn't that sound more respectable than "lying"?) has become such a common practice in the United States that people who do not embellish their records are at a distinct disadvantage in competing for jobs. And prospective employers are being warned on TV news that taking résumés at face value is foolish and naive.

What about time budgets in the service industries? One year, for example, an accountant claims on his time report that a particular client's work took ten hours. The next year, someone else coming up in the firm wants to look good, so even though the job still took ten hours, the aspiring young accountant records eight. The third year, eight is the budgeted number. When the job still takes ten, what does this year's accountant do? She can't afford to blow the budget, and she needs to look good at evaluation time, too, so in the third year she records seven and one-half. Either the firm "eats" those hours or the accountant, in effect, donates them for the sake of career advancement. Of course, eventually, someone has to take the fall for this lying because the budget can't be "beat" every year, or after a while the accountants would finish the work before they ever got to the client's office. But, boy, does it look good while the game lasts!

Lying is not just a bad habit. It is a symptom of heart disease, for it is the heart that harbors either bitterness and deceit or godly values.

Our culture does encourage and reward lying. In fact, we've reached the point when, as a recent *Time* magazine essay stated: "[Our culture is] a huckstering, show-bizzy world, jangling with hype, hullabaloo, and hooey, bull, baloney, and bamboozle-ment." But our affinity for deceit goes deeper than society's pressures. As the prophet Jeremiah said, "The heart is deceitful above all things" (Jeremiah 17:9). Dr. Leonard Keeler, the inventor of the lie detector machine, interviewed and studied over twenty-five thousand people in his research, and his findings led him to conclude that people are basically dishonest. There is something deep within our nature that draws us to deception.

Lying is not just a bad habit. It is a symptom of heart disease, for it is the heart that harbors either bitterness and deceit or godly values. The mouth only gives expression to the thoughts given it by our inmost being. As Jesus said, "How can you who are evil say anything good? For out of the overflow of the heart the mouth speaks. The good man brings good things out of the good stored up in him, and the evil man brings evil things out of the evil stored up in him" (Matthew 12:34, 35).

Long before Jesus' attack on the Pharisees, though, the Proverbs had taught the connection between the state of the heart and the fruit of the mouth: "Above all else, guard your heart, for it is the wellspring of life. Put away perversity from your mouth; keep corrupt talk far from your lips" (Proverbs 4:23, 24). Also, "The tongue of the righteous is choice silver, but the heart of the wicked is of little value" (10:20). And, "The discerning heart seeks knowledge, but the mouth of a fool feeds on folly" (15:14).

We excuse what comes from our mouths as just a "slip of the tongue." But God says it is a slip of the heart.

Here's the point: Too often, we excuse what comes from our mouths, whether it is deceitful or simply hurtful words, as just a "slip of the tongue." But God says it is a slip of the heart. Our tongues have let some of the ugliness that we try to keep hidden inside slip into public view. People lie because they have deceit in their hearts—a battle lost in a war that has been raging since Eden.

To Whom?

Lying to Our Neighbors

To whom do we lie? The first group is pretty easy to identify, isn't it? We lie to our neighbors—to those God has placed around us. We all remember that nursery rhyme that says, "Sticks and stones may break my bones, but words will never hurt me." But that's just not true. Words can destroy us. They can fracture our lives.

There are a lot of ways to hurt others through lying. There's perjury, of course. And there's also

slander and gossip. There is a rather tongue-in-
cheek definition of gossip that says gossip is saying
something you like about someone you don't. That
pretty much hits the nail on the head, doesn't it? A
preacher once did a study to determine what sin the
Bible confronts most often. What would you guess?
Murder? Adultery? Try slander and gossip. The
Bible condemns these misuses of the tongue more
than any other sin. I personally think that they have
destroyed more churches than any other sin.

Gossip is saying something you like about someone you don't.

There are other ways to hurt our neighbors by
misusing our tongues, too. Insinuation is a powerful
weapon in the war of words; plus, it carries the
added bonus of being a no-risk lie. All I have to do is
wonder aloud to someone else how so-and-so got all
their money, or why you-know-who is so popular, or
how such-and-such got that promotion, and the
damage has begun. I haven't even had to accuse
them of a thing. Insinuation is a favorite tool of the
devil, by the way. "Did God *really* say you can't eat
from that tree?" "Does Job fear God for *nothing?*" "*If*
you are the Son of God . . ." Satan loves to insinuate.

Flattery is also a form of lying. I'm not talking
about encouraging people, but about saying something to soften them up so that we can get something
from them in return. A proverb says the person who
flatters is spreading a net at your feet—he's setting
a trap (Proverbs 29:5).

Another way we sometimes lie to others is by
remaining silent. In other words, I lie to you when I
keep from you truth that will help you. For instance,

when Grover Cleveland was a boy, his neighbor's
hen laid an egg in Grover's yard every day. Now,
Grover could have just said nothing and used the
egg himself. After all, he did find the egg in his own
yard. But every day Grover insisted upon returning
the egg to his neighbor. If only our politicians today
could be so honest.

That's not to say that we should express every
thought that enters our heads, of course. That would
be like the woman who came to John Wesley one
time and said, "I think I know the talent God has
given me!" Wesley replied, "Yes, ma'am? What is the
gift?" And the woman said, "I think it is to always
speak my mind." Wesley thought a moment, then
replied, "I do not think God would mind if you buried
that talent." We are not to hammer people with
truth. But we are not to deprive them of it either.

Lying to God

All deception is an affront to God, for his nature is
the epitome of truth. "It is impossible for God to lie"
(Hebrews 6:18). His insistence on the truth helps
explain the example he made of Ananias and
Sapphira in Acts 5. You probably remember that
this couple sold some land and donated part of the
proceeds for the welfare of the Christians in Jerusalem. The only problem was that they told the church
there they had given *all* the money from the sale of
the land. Peter confronted them and said, "How is it
that Satan has so filled your hearts that you have
lied to the Holy Spirit? . . . You have not lied to men
but to God."

It's hard to imagine how anyone could attempt to
deceive God . . . or is it? Have you ever known anyone who tried to get the benefits of the gospel without accepting the cost of the Cross? We call people
like that hypocrites, but God just calls them liars.

I'm convinced that hypocrisy among people who
wear God's name has hurt his reputation among
unbelievers more than any other sin. So many of the
TV evangelists and hyped-up "ministries" that have
gained notoriety in recent years have been exposed
as frauds—self-serving con men out to get an easy
buck—who have, in the minds of the unchurched,
caused a cloud of suspicion to hang over even the
legitimate churches in this country. By the way, a
person does not have to have a television contract to
show unbelieving people a hypocritical spirit. Pre-
tending to be what you're not—especially when you
are doing it in God's name—is a hideous evil.

Lying to Ourselves

We are experts at lying to ourselves, aren't we? "I
don't have a drinking problem." "It's not hurting
anybody but me." "I can stop anytime I want." Or,
one I hear a lot, "I don't go to church anymore, but
I've never been closer to God." Come on, folks!

We lie to ourselves when we don't want to face the
truth about the evil with which we choose to live.
John writes,

> If we claim to be without sin, we deceive our-
> selves and the truth is not in us. If we confess
> our sins, he is faithful and just and will forgive
> us our sins and purify us from all unrighteous-
> ness. If we claim we have not sinned, we make
> him out to be a liar and his word has no place
> in our lives (1 John 1:8-10).

We've got to remember that sin is not an overpow-
ering obstacle for God, but our denying our sin is.
Religion is fertile ground for self-deception, for we
can easily go to church a little bit, listen to a little

preaching, sing a song or two, hear a prayer or two, and try to convince ourselves we're pretty good people when, in reality, our hearts are full of hatred and hypocrisy. As James wrote, "Do not merely listen to the word, and so deceive yourselves. Do what it says" (James 1:22).

How Now?

How can we start now to begin living honestly with our God, our neighbors, and ourselves? Here are four suggestions:

1. Monitor Your Heart

The heart is the source of everything we say. It's possible over time to become a chronic deceiver and not even be aware of our problem. We spend so much time trying to position ourselves to obtain the best possible image in the minds of those around us that we lose sight of the fact that we are not only living with deception, we are in its grasp, and the truth has become a stranger to us.

How do we avoid this pitfall? We give the Holy Spirit opportunities to work in us to change our nature. We pray, study the Bible, and participate in worship of the God of truth. We also make ourselves accountable to other people of character. We open up our lives to them so that, if falsehood should try to take root in our hearts, they are close enough to us to see the danger and alert us to it. Of course, we must submit ourselves to routine, exacting self-examinations, asking ourselves, "How honest was I today?" Doing so can be painful, but it's far less so than letting deceit take hold in our lives and being lost eternally (Revelation 21:8).

If we will do these things sincerely, I believe that God will begin to take control of our hearts so that when we begin to lie, the Holy Spirit will alert us to what we're doing and help us back up and speak the truth. If we don't do these things, however, we're going to quench the Spirit by refusing him opportunity to work in our lives, and we'll find ourselves growing comfortable in the presence of deceit.

2. Diet on Wholesome Conversation

I believe we are too prone to listen to and talk about ugliness. How many of us buy those magazines whose sole purpose for existence is to spread rumor and insinuation? How many of us watch television programs whose basic appeal to the audience is to spread the latest gossip or to discuss the horrible, sensational problems of sick people and their relationships? If that is our diet, how can we be developing the kind of character that loves truth?

We've got to be more dedicated to promoting the honor and reputation of others. Paul said, "Whatever is true, whatever is noble, whatever is right, whatever is pure, whatever is lovely, whatever is admirable—if anything is excellent or praiseworthy—think about such things" (Philippians 4:8). You can't consume garbage and develop character.

> *You can't consume garbage and develop character.*

3. Encourage Others

The apostle Paul gives us good advice when he says, "Do not let any unwholesome talk come out of your mouths, but only what is helpful for building others up according to their needs, that it may benefit those who listen. And do not grieve the Holy Spirit of God, with whom you were sealed for the day of redemption" (Ephesians 4:29, 30).

We need to take every opportunity to speak good instead of evil words. Too often in church, the only teaching we hear about the tongue is to avoid misusing it, but God gave us the power of speech in order for us to use it for good in his world. He wants his people of character to speak out. He wants us to speak out in society, in our schools, in our neighborhoods, and in our homes so that people who don't have their hearts tuned to him can hear his voice through our words. He wants us to talk about justice, mercy, and love, and about a God who has a plan for how people can live lives of character so that they can be at peace with themselves, with each other, and with him.

4. Consider Your Reflection

God never intended deceit to be part of his world. It was introduced by Satan. And just as Satan used deceit in the Garden to place a wide gap between God and the people he created, Satan is still trying to use this tool to distance us from each other and from our God. Jesus, speaking of the devil, says, "When he lies, he speaks his native language, for he is a liar and the father of lies" (John 8:44b). Just as all truth is from God, all lies are from Satan. The devil spews deceit over the cosmos, and the ninth principle in God's plan for building character can be truly understood only in light of the tremendous struggle taking place between God's army and Satan's: the forces of truth versus the army of deceit.

Paul describes this spiritual warfare:

> The god of this age has blinded the minds of unbelievers, so that they cannot see the light of the gospel of the glory of Christ, who is the image of God. For God, who said, "Let light

shine out of darkness," made his light shine in
our hearts to give us the light of the knowledge
of the glory of God in the face of Christ"
(2 Corinthians 4:4, 6).

We are caught up in something infinitely bigger
than ourselves. There is a struggle going on in the
cosmos—call it light versus darkness, call it good
versus evil, call it truth versus falsehood—but it all
comes down to this: it's God versus Satan. Satan
wants us to become victims of lies, and he wants us
to victimize others with lies, as well. That is why, if
we are going to enter this struggle on the side of
truth, we've got to enter it at the core of our beings.
It will mean not only a change of behavior but also a
change of nature.

Ephesians 4:22-24 tells us, "You were taught, with
regard to your former way of life, to put off your old
self, which is being corrupted by its deceitful desires;
to be made new in the attitude of your minds; and to
put on the new self, created to be like God in true
righteousness and holiness." What's the first thing
that happens when the Holy Spirit changes our
natures? Verse 25 explains, "Therefore each of you
must put off falsehood and speak truthfully to his
neighbor, for we are all members of one body."

Paul repeats this idea of exchanging the old deceitful nature that belonged to Satan for the new
truthful one that belongs to God. He says, "Do not lie
to each other, since you have taken off your old self
with its practices and have put on the new self,
which is being renewed in knowledge in the image of
its Creator" (Colossians 3:9, 10).

Reflecting the image of our Creator—isn't that
what it really means to be people of character? We're
just reflectors. Now, reflectors can be as beautiful as
they are useful. The moon, for instance, gives off no

light of its own. There's nothing especially glorious
about it, except that it always faces an object that is
glorious: the sun. And because the sun lets its light
shine on the moon and the moon is positioned to
receive that light, it shines as a beacon in the
night—a light to an otherwise dark world. People of
character reflect God's character. And part of his
very essence is truth. Only when we reflect his truth
can we build communities and families where respect and trust abound.

All in Truth

When the father of the great Emmanuel Kant was
an old man, he made a dangerous trip through the
forests of Poland to his native country of Silesia. On
the way he encountered robbers who demanded his
valuables, finally asking, "Have you given us all?"
and only letting him go when he answered, "All."

When safely out of their sight, his hand touched
something hard in the hem of his robe. It was his
gold, sewn there for safety and quite forgotten by
him in his fear and confusion.

At once he hurried back to find the robbers, and
having found them, he said meekly, "I have told you
what was not true; it was unintentional. I was too
terrified to think. Here, take the gold in my robes."

Then, to the old man's astonishment, nobody
offered to take his gold. After a moment, one robber
went and brought back his purse. Another robber
restored his book of prayer, while still another led
his horse toward him and helped him to mount.
They then all asked for his blessing and watched
him slowly ride away.

Truth had triumphed over thievery. Truth will
always triumph in the end.

Focusing Your Faith

1. Lies are not always told with words. How else do you see Americans lie?

2. What is the most deceptive kind of lie—the one furthest or closest to the truth? Why?

3. What lies do you hear people tell in the name of "politeness" or "compassion"? When is withholding the truth wrong? Right?

4. Satan is identified as "the father of lies." What are some of his favorites that you hear?

5. What are your most common self-deceptions?

6. How do you view Kant's father for correcting his "lie" and giving the robbers his hidden gold? What experience have you had when truth _didn't_ triumph?

7. What is the most memorable lesson you have learned about the value of truth? What is the best way to teach truthfulness to someone else?

Chapter 12

The High Price of Plenty

On the night of
November 16, 1930,
Mrs. Henrietta Garrett,
a lonely 81-year-old
widow, died in her
home in Philadelphia
and, unwillingly,
started the most fan-
tastic case of inherit-
ance litigation in history.

> **Principle 10:**
>
> *Be Content*
>
> *Exodus 20:17*
> *Philippians 4:11-13*

She had failed to leave a will, or no will was found,
to her $17 million estate: a mystery left unsolved.
She had expertly handled her financial affairs since
the death of her husband in 1895 and, therefore, she
must have realized that, without a will, her fortune
would become involved in many legal battles.

Although Mrs. Garrett had, at the time of her
death, only one known living relative, a second
cousin, and less than a dozen friends, attempts to

prove relationship to her and to claim a part or all of her estate have since been made by more than 26,000 persons from 47 states and 29 foreign countries, represented by more than 3,000 lawyers.

In their frantic efforts, these alleged relatives have committed perjury, faked family records, changed their own names, altered data in church Bibles, and concocted absurd tales of illegitimacy. As a result, twelve were fined, ten received jail sentences, two committed suicide, and three were murdered. The estate has, in the meantime, increased to $30 million.

All of this bedlam came from discontented people—people who are not happy with what they have. God knew that lack of contentment would be a major problem for people. So, that's where his tenth instruction for happy living originated.

"We have paid a high spiritual price for our plenty."

Sometime ago there appeared in a newspaper a cartoon showing two fields divided by a fence. Both fields were about the same size, and each had plenty of the same kind of grass, green and lush.

In each field there was a mule, and each mule had his head through the fence eating grass from the other mule's pasture. All around each mule in his own field was plenty of grass, yet the grass in the other field seemed greener or fresher, although it was harder to get. In the process the mules were caught in the wires. The cartoonist put just one word at the bottom of the picture—"DISCONTENT"!

Euell Gibbons, well-known commentator and author, observed "We live in a vastly complex society which has been able to provide us with a multitude of material things, and this is good, but people are beginning to suspect that we have paid a high spiritual price for our plenty." And I couldn't agree more.

When I was a boy, I loved going to my grandparents' house. It was a young boy's paradise. Among the many places there where my brother, cousins, and I liked to play, our favorite was a huge oak tree. This was no ordinary oak tree, mind you. It was a giant among oak trees, and it was perfect for climbing. And, man, it was strong! We were sure it could hold anything we could hoist onto its branches. How we loved that old oak tree!

One night during one of my summer visits, a thunderstorm blew in. It wasn't a major storm, just some wind and rain. But when we awoke the next morning, that very ordinary storm had felled our giant oak tree. It was inconceivable to us how such a paltry wind could have overcome this magnificent tree. That is, it was inconceivable until we were able to look at the tree close-up.

As it turned out, our tree that looked so mighty from the outside, that had been able to support us and our treasures with such ease, had been hollow—its insides had been eaten out by insects and disease. All it took was a little storm to break through its appearance of strength and expose the weakness within.

Although I was too young to make the application then, as an adult I've often thought of that oak tree as I looked at lives brought down by hidden sin. Despite how beautiful and "together" our lives look on the outside, the strength of our character, like the strength of that tree, is directly related to what is inside us. And our society is eaten up inside by being dissatisfied with what we have. We are paying a high spiritual price for our plenty.

Because the underlying causes of sin lie within us, laws regulating only external behavior can never get to the root of the sin problem. This is why, after he gave us all his instructions about how we are to behave, the Lord finishes his Code of Ethics with a principle about how we are to think:

> *You shall not covet your neighbor's house. You shall not covet your neighbor's wife, or his manservant or maidservant, his ox or donkey, or anything that belongs to your neighbor* (Exodus 20:17).

While the principle of putting God first supplies the motivation for obeying all the others, the tenth principle of not coveting supplies the explanation of why we disobey all the others. Take King David, for example. When David became involved with Bathsheba, the Bible tells us that he ignored the eighth principle when he stole another man's wife. He ignored the seventh principle when he committed adultery with her. He ignored the ninth when he lied about his affair with the woman and the third principle when the whole thing took the Lord's name in vain. He ignored the sixth when he arranged for the murder of Bathsheba's husband, and he ignored the first principle because God wasn't the center of his heart through the whole business.

David ignored seven of God's ten instructions for happy living! Why? Because he ignored the tenth principle first. Out of his discontentment, he had an unhealthy desire for his neighbor's wife. The tenth principle makes clear what the other nine have been assuming: that sin lies in the heart long before it shows in the hands.

Consider the minister caught in an extra-marital affair, the Sunday school teacher brought down by

her own jealousy of and gossip about another, the
Christian family members not speaking to one
another because someone feels cheated by Mama's or
Daddy's will. These are all examples of people who
may have protected and cultivated their Christian
facade successfully for years (perhaps fooling even
themselves), but who have fallen victim to the same
inner sickness. They were covetous. They wanted in
an unhealthy way what they didn't have. They, like
David, certainly never intended to let this "go so
far." But once we accept dissatisfaction in our
hearts, the enemy has gained a foothold, and it is
hard to stop the sinning. You cannot develop character in the heart that covets.

> **_Sin lies in the heart long before it_
> _shows in the hands._**

What is "coveting"? The meaning of the word used
in the text is simply "an enthusiastic desire," and it
was originally morally neutral. People have always
had desires, of course, and the behavior we choose to
call coveting has a great deal to do with the general
thought within our culture on the appropriateness of
desires. Some religions say, "Abandon yourself to
desires. Whatever you want, go for it." Hedonism
says, "You only go around once in life, so grab for all
the gusto you can." On the other hand, religions such
as Buddhism take the opposite approach, saying
that all desire is evil. "The problem with the world,"
they say, "is desire. So learn to quench desire."
    God, however, has never stood for either of these
extremes. In fact, He has placed certain desires
within us. My desire for a lifelong mate was God-
given. Jamie's and my desire to become parents was

God-given, too. Neither was wrong. However, if I had let my desire for a mate lead me to try to take the wife of another, or if my desire for children had led me to resent God's giving children to our friends and family before he gave them to us, I would have perverted the good desires God gave us into something unhealthy and sinful—into covetousness.

The Cause of Covetousness: Resentment

The root of coveting is dissatisfaction with God's allotment of things. We resent what we think is the unfairness of God (maybe we call it the unfairness of life) and, because of that internal resentment, we act in some way that dishonors God. Because Cain resented the fact that his sacrifice to God was not as acceptable as Abel's, his resentment boiled up into the murder of his brother. God warned Cain saying, "Sin is crouching at your door; it desires to have you, but you must master it" (Genesis 4:7). Obviously, Abel's sin of coveting resulted in his breaking of another of God's instructions. When Saul resented the praise heaped on David, his resentment erupted in anger, hatred, rage, and attempts at murder. And Ahab resented that little vineyard that Naboth owned to the point that Ahab's wife, Jezebel, cheated and plotted murder to get it for him.

One of the Bible's most interesting examples of how resentment and unhealthy desires can hurt is in Luke 15. This is the story we usually call the "Prodigal Son." However, Jesus' point in the story is that there were two lost sons. The younger one openly rebels and leaves home, but, after a time, returns home penitently, and is restored to his father. The older son, meanwhile, has stayed with his father all this time and, to all appearances, has been a faithful and loving child. When he returns from working in the fields and hears the rejoicing at the homecoming party for his brother, the elder son asks a servant, "What's happening?" The servant tells him his lost brother is back, and his father is throwing a party. How does the elder son react? As soon as the father comes out to talk to him, the son states his case: "I've slaved for you all these years, and you never threw me a party!" He resents the attention and honor his father is giving the younger son because he believes he is more deserving of such treatment than his brother. He didn't leave home, but covetousness put a great distance between him and his father.

It reminds me of a story of Abraham Lincoln. (Have you ever noticed how his name keeps popping up when you talk about people of character?) Abe was walking down the street one day with his two young sons, both of whom were crying. "What's the matter with your boys?" asked a passerby.

"Exactly what is wrong with the whole world," said Lincoln. "I have three walnuts, and each boy wants two."

One reason Jesus told the parable of the prodigal son was for the benefit of the elder brothers of his day, the Pharisees. He wanted them to see that they were being eaten up inside by their resentment of the attention that God gives to the lost. They didn't believe that "sinners" deserved God's love, but they felt that they had *earned* it.

Of course, it would be hard to find any modern day "elder brothers". . . or would it? Church growth experts say that almost always when an existing church tries to make changes designed to reach the lost in its community, the strongest criticism comes from people within the church who feel that, since they are the ones who have given that congregation their time and money, the congregation should be focused on meeting their needs and not some stranger's. Resentment can rear its ugly head any-where—even among God's people.

The Consequence of Covetousness: Estrangement

So, covetousness is a very old problem with very timeless consequences. One is distance between us and our neighbors. Did you notice that the tenth principle is more than just four words long? It doesn't just say, "You shall not covet"; it says, "You shall not covet *your neighbor's*" this or that. Coveting comes between us and the people God wants us to love and serve. James analyzes the problem quite concisely:

> What causes fights and quarrels among you? Don't they come from your desires that battle within you? You want something but don't get it. You kill and covet, but you cannot have what you want. You quarrel and fight. You do not have, because you do not ask God. When you ask, you do not receive, because you ask with wrong motives, that you may spend what you get on your pleasures (James 4:1-3).

Why are there wars in the world? Why are there so many fights in the world? Why is there so much violence, tension, and discord in the world? Why so many divorces? Why so many fractured families and friendships? James says the answer is quite simple: we want what we can't have; so, we fight and quar-rel about it.

But not only does coveting distance us from oth-ers, it puts a gulf between us and God as well. For coveting is ultimately worshiping our own desires, and that is a violation of the first principle. Coveting turns goods into gods. If you think I'm stating the case too strongly, look at what Paul writes: "Be sure of this, that no fornicator or impure man, or one who is covetous (that is, an idolater), has any inheritance in the kingdom of Christ and of God" (Ephesians 5:5, RSV). Or look at Paul's warning to "put to death therefore what is earthly in you: fornication, impurity, passion, evil desire, and covetousness, which is idolatry. On account of these the wrath of God is coming" (Colossians 3:5, 6, RSV).

Coveting turns goods into gods.

Covetousness is idolatry because it places a substitute for God, a false god, in our hearts. God created each of us with desires—desires that only he can satisfy. He created us to long for him and to want him and to be unfulfilled until we find him. As the adage says, "Every person has a God-shaped vacuum within." But covetousness is trying to satisfy those needs with something or someone else. Charles Spurgeon was an evangelist who converted many, many people, but he once said, "I never knew a covetous man to be converted." Why? A covetous heart has no room for God. So, once again, we come back to that foundation of God's principles: Put God first.

The Cure for Covetousness: Contentment

Our quest for character is thwarted until we are willing to face up to what's inside us and deal with the disease. The first step is detection. There are two questions that can help us assess our heart condition:

1.   What Do I Think about Most of the Time?

This question is important, because what we think about is what we desire, and what we desire is what we will become. There is a story about a preacher who dropped by rather unexpectedly to visit a family from his congregation. The mother of the house, wanting to make a good impression, said to her young daughter, "Honey, why don't you go and get that Good Book that we all love so much." So the little girl ran off to the next room and came back with a big smile, carrying the Sears catalog. This family had obviously substituted the Wish Book for the Good Book.

People of character pay attention to Paul's call: "Since, then, you have been raised with Christ, set your hearts on things above, where Christ is seated at the right hand of God. Set your minds on things above, not on earthly things" (Colossians 3:1, 2). And Paul is certainly not alone in encouraging us to desire the things of heaven. The Today's English Version translates Christ's words like this: "Happy are those whose greatest desire is to do what God requires; God will satisfy them fully!" (Matthew 5:6). That's a promise you can take to the bank, folks!

G.K. Chesterton put it this way, "There are two ways to get enough; one is to continue to accumulate more and more. The other is to desire less and less." And God is always there to help you control your desires.

2.   How Good Am I at Rejoicing with Others?

Did you realize rejoicing with others is a command? Romans 12:15 says, "Rejoice with those who rejoice; mourn with those who mourn." And I must confess that, at times, the first half of that command is harder for me to obey than the second half. I don't

have any problem mourning with you when you have
suffered a great loss, but when you have received a
great blessing I haven't received yet, the rejoicing
part is a little hard.

Let's be honest. When a popular single man or
woman at church decides to get married, is the
engaged one usually congratulated with open arms
by the people he or she "beat out" for the prize?
Maybe. But often, behind the couple's back, there is
gossip and innuendo because others in the singles'
group resent the pair's happiness together.

And when one woman in a group of friends begins
losing the weight that they've all been talking about
losing for years, do the others celebrate with her?
Sometimes. But sometimes, when she's not present,
her "friends" wonder aloud if she's been "taking
shots" to lose the weight (surely it's not willpower) or
if she'll really be able to keep it off (probably not).

What about the guy who drives up to church in a
new car? I've been in the group when the guy walks
up, thrilled with his new acquisition, and someone
else says something like, "How much mileage do you
get? Really? Mine's better."

It's not always easy to rejoice with those who
rejoice. There is a legend of a Burmese potter who
was jealous of the success of a washerman's profit-
able trade. The potter's jealousy led him to persuade
the king that if this washerman was so good, he
should be able to take one of the king's elephants
and wash it so well it would become white.

But when the king made the request of the
washerman, he replied that according to the customs
of his trade, anything he washed must be in a vessel.
So the king instructed the potter to make a vessel in
which the washerman could wash the elephant.

The potter made the biggest washpot he could,
but, of course, as soon as the elephant stepped into

the pot, it crumbled into a thousand pieces. Over and over again the potter tried to make a vessel that could hold the elephant. Eventually, it was his own business that he destroyed by his covetousness.

The moral is pretty obvious, of course. We can either rejoice with others at their blessings or be ruined by our resentment of their success.

Defeating the Disease

The only way the Bible teaches to remove resentment is to cultivate contentment. Paul wrote to Timothy, "But godliness with contentment is great gain. For we brought nothing into the world, and we can take nothing out of it. But if we have food and clothing, we will be content with that" (1 Timothy 6:6-8). Godliness is what we strive for when we seek to live by principles one through nine. Contentment, however, is what we are shooting for in number ten. The Bible says that the formula for living a truly rich life—a life of character—is to walk consistently by God's pattern and his power, accompanied by an attitude of inner satisfaction with his will for our lives.

Ed Young, a minister in Houston, Texas, tells a story about a fellow he knew back when Young preached in North Carolina. The fellow's name was Tommy, and he was a respected member of his church. Tommy had only finished the third grade, but he had spent his life reading and studying the Bible. He was the favorite adult Sunday school teacher, and because he had done so much over the course of his life for the community and church, the congregation wanted to send Tommy on a trip.

Now, Tommy had been raised in that little town in North Carolina and had never been more than fifty miles from home, but they collected enough money to

send him to New York City for five days. When
Tommy came back, Ed Young asked him what he
thought of New York. Tommy summed it up by
saying, "Ed, the last night I was there, I got down on
my knees by the bed, and I said, 'Lord, I thank you
that I have not seen anything that I want.' "

Godliness is what we strive for when we
seek to live by principles one through
nine. Contentment, however, is what we
are shooting for in number ten.

That kind of contentment is not inherited. It is
cultivated. It's not that some people are born con-
tented and others aren't. Contentment is a discipline
of the mind, and it's developed through practice and
prayer. Paul said, "I have learned to be content
whatever the circumstances. I know what it is to be
in need, and I know what it is to have plenty. I have
learned the secret of being content in any and every
situation. I can do everything through him who gives
me strength" (Philippians 4:11-13). If we want to live
that kind of life, we must set ourselves on a course of
learning to live it.

What is the cure for coveting? Contentment. The
key to defeating the disease is learning to be satisfied with what God has given us and not needing
more than that to be happy. If we don't learn contentment, we will learn covetousness, and it will eat
at us until we find ourselves not following the other
instructions for living. But how can we cultivate
contentment in our lives?

Learn the Difference Between *Wants* and *Needs*

Paul tells Timothy that if he just has food and

clothing, he is content. The word in the Greek that is translated "clothing" here may also include the idea of shelter, so, giving us the benefit of the doubt, we'll include that, too. But, think about it for a minute. How many of us can honestly say we believe our needs are that simple?

I have always enjoyed the story of the Quaker gentleman who was watching as a new neighbor moved in next door. The Quakers are a people known for the simple lifestyle they have adopted, but the new neighbor obviously had chosen a different path. As the Quaker watched load after load of fine, exquisite furniture and paintings being taken into the house, he called across to his neighbor, "Friend, if thee hath need of anything, come and see me, and I will teach thee how to live without it." We should all learn from him.

So, if we have the essentials for living—food, clothing, and a place to live where we're sheltered from the wet and cold—Paul says we've got enough to call ourselves rich. And, in truth, that would give us more material security than the Lord Jesus had on earth. Remember, he had no place to lay his head.

Tragically, there are people in this world, even people in our communities, who do not have these essentials for living. But most of us have these and more. Our problem isn't finding a coat to wear; it's deciding *which* coat to wear. We don't worry about if we'll eat tonight, but what kind of food we'll choose. And rather than being concerned about being without a place to sleep, we're consumed with whether our home is as nice as those of the people with whom we associate.

A little plaque hangs on the wall in our study. Jamie bought it back in the years when we were wanting and waiting for children. It says, "Contentment is not the fulfillment of what you want, but the realization of how much you already have." Considering all God has given us, shouldn't rejoicing rather than resenting characterize our lives?

Learn the Difference Between *Temporary* and *Eternal*

The story is told that an American Jew visiting the land of his parents went to see the famous teacher Rabbi Chaim. When the American entered the home of the rabbi, he was amazed at the stark living conditions there. All that Chaim had was a table, a bench, and a little pallet. Appalled, the American asked, "Rabbi, where is all your furniture?" The Rabbi responded, "Where is all *your* furniture?" The tourist said, "I don't have any furniture with me. I'm just traveling through." To which the Rabbi replied, "So am I." This is just a temporary home for all of us, isn't it?

Paul tells us that "we brought nothing into this world, and we can take nothing out of it," but it seems that's a hard lesson for people to learn. I read with some interest a story of the aftermath of John D. Rockefeller's death. It seems one particular journalist was absolutely obsessed with determining how much Rockefeller was worth at the time of his death, so he set up an appointment with one of Rockefeller's top aides. The reporter asked him, "How much money did Rockefeller leave behind?" The aide replied simply, "All of it." We didn't enter this world coveting anything, and we won't leave this world with anything we coveted.

Jesus taught his followers to take an eternal viewpoint:

> One of the multitude said to him, "Teacher, bid my brother divide the inheritance with me."
>
> But he said to him, "Man, who made me a

judge or divider over you?"

And he said to them, "Take heed, and beware of all covetousness; for a man's life does not consist in the abundance of his possessions" (Luke 12:13, RSV).

Paul gives the same advice: "So we fix our eyes not on what is seen, but on what is unseen. For what is seen is temporary, but what is unseen is eternal" (2 Corinthians 4:18).

I hope by now one thing, at least, is completely clear to you: God's instructions for living are more than just a call to conform to some external code of behavior. Far from it! They are a claim to God's right to rule in the realm of our attitudes. The tenth principle says the quest for character starts on the inside. If we keep our hands from sin but fail to guard our hearts, we are losing in our quest for character!

People of character do not envy others' temporal blessings. People of character desire eternal blessings, so they are willing to face internal issues. It makes sense, doesn't it, that God's law is the only law in history against coveting. How could man police such a law? How could we know what's inside another? But God knows our hearts, and he wants our hearts to belong only to him.

Focusing Your Faith

1. Can you name two contemporary songs or movies that show how discontented Americans are?

2. "Sin lies in the heart long before it shows in the hands." What do you see Americans doing with their hands that indicates they have discontented hearts?

3. When you are bored or lonely, what do you do to cheer yourself up? Does spending money make you feel better or worse? Why?

4. "Coveting turns goods into gods." How do you see people living out this statement?

5. Have you ever heard someone confess the sin of covetousness? Why are we hesitant to admit a problem we all struggle with?

6. How good are you at rejoicing with others who have good fortune?

7. Think of an example of someone you know who has learned to be content. How did they become content?

Chapter 13

Revival
at Sinai

᎒

The mighty prophet
Elijah had been on a
spiritual high for two or
three years. At Elijah's
word, rain had stopped
falling on the earth for
three years, and only
his word could make
the rain fall again. God

> ### Return to the Summit
>
> *1 Kings 19*
> *Romans 13:8-10*

had personally cared for Elijah by sending food in
the beaks of ravens to him at the Kerith Ravine. He
had raised a young boy from death through Elijah.
With God's help Elijah had destroyed the 450 prophets of Baal and the 400 prophets of Asherah on
Mount Carmel. Then God had empowered him to
outrun King Ahab for twenty-three miles into
Jezreel. He was surely riding high on his spiritual
success.

Then Elijah received a threatening message from

Queen Jezebel, which said she was going to have
him killed by the next day for what he had done to
her prophets. Crash! Elijah fell from his spiritual
high to an all-time low. He was terrified and ran for
his life. He sank into the pits of depression. He ran
all the way to Beersheba and then another full day's
journey into the desert. Finally, he flopped down
under a broom tree and prayed that he would die.

"I've had enough, Lord," said Elijah. "Take my life.
I'm no better than my ancestors." He had concluded
that his work was fruitless and, so, life was no
longer worth living. He had lost his confidence in the
triumph of the kingdom of God and was withdrawing
from the battle. He thought there was no hope for
the next generation of God's people.

An interesting thing happened at this point of the
story. God gently cared for his discouraged servant
by sending an angel to feed him. He gave him rest
and food to prepare him for the journey he was about
to take—a journey back to God's mountain, a journey back to the Sinai Summit.

When Elijah was refreshed, God sustained him for
forty days and nights while he traveled back to the
summit. That's the same amount of time God sustained Moses on the mountain where the summit
originally took place. And it's the same amount of
time God sustained Jesus in the desert later when
he faced Satan. God had not deserted his people.

Elijah climbed the mountain alone to face God.
Then God gently whispered to him, "Elijah, what are
you doing here?"

Elijah condemned the Israelites before God for
having rejected the Code of Ethics God had given
them at the summit. He announced to God that he
alone remained faithful to him, and he complained
about the fruitlessness of his many years of hard
work for God. He had lost faith in the power of God's

principles to solve the world's character crisis. He
wanted out; he was tired; he thought God's solutions
had failed and that the world could not be cured of
its fatal ailment.

It was there on the mountain of God, at the summit of Sinai that God restored Elijah's confidence
and faith. He showed Elijah that he was not alone in
his fight to recharacter the world. Over seven thousand other faithful servants were on his side, doing
battle daily with Elijah to rebuild the character of
God's people. Then he sent Elijah back into the war
to continue his combat with Satan for the souls of
the next generation of God's people.

A Hole in the Moral Ozone?

"There is a hole in the moral ozone, and it is probably getting bigger," says the head of the Josephson
Institute for the Advancement of Ethics, a nonprofit,
Los Angeles-based group devoted to character educa-
tion. According to the institute, an "unacceptably
high" number of fifteen to thirty year olds are willing
to steal, lie, and cheat at work and in school.

This report was based on a study of detailed inter-
views during 1991–92 with nine thousand young
people and adults (nearly seven thousand of which
were high schoolers and college students).

The findings of that report were scary. A third of
high school students and 16 percent of college students admit that they have stolen something from a
store in the past year. Nearly two-thirds of high
school students and a third of college students admit
to cheating on an exam within the past year. More
than a third of all high school and college students
said they would lie on a résumé or job application to
get a job. And 21 percent of college students indi-
cated that they would falsify a report if it were

necessary to keep a job.

Here's the good news: By no means are young people "moral mutants." They're simply mimicking and escalating others' character behavior. Bad news: "We're creating a society where cheaters prosper, and you can't honestly tell children that honesty is the best policy," contends the institute's executive vice-president. "Although there is no way of proving that young people's ethics of today are worse than those in the past, they are bad enough to cause concern."

There is hope for America's character crisis.

Gang violence. Sexual "freedom." Racial hatred. Chaos in classrooms. The line between right and wrong is often blurred for kids today. Their focus on God's ethics is blurred by the examples they see of his ethics being ignored by their parents, teachers, and work supervisors. They are mimicking us. So, it's up to us to help sharpen their focus.

The fact is, God's solutions to the world's character crisis are still valid. His principles have not failed, we have just failed to apply them. Like Elijah, we must return to the summit and commit ourselves to joining with others in the struggle for the soul of our land. There is hope for America's character crisis.

Beginning the Journey Back

Where does the journey back to God's mountain begin? It begins with God's greatest instruction of all.

Jesus had a number of opportunities in his teaching ministry to give us insight into the heart of God's

Code of Ethics. For example, "One of the teachers of
the law came and heard them debating. Noticing
that Jesus had given them a good answer, he asked
him, 'Of all the commandments, which is the most
important?' " (Mark 12:28).

That's a great question, isn't it? And the question
didn't just appear out of a vacuum either. The rabbis
had debated the relative importance of the commandments for a long time, and out of these rabbini-
cal debates had developed a system which catego-
rized laws as either "heavy laws" or "light laws."

What the teacher of the law was asking Jesus
was, "What is the heaviest of the heavy laws?" Jesus
answered:

> "The most important one . . . is this: 'Hear, O
> Israel, the Lord our God, the Lord is one. Love
> the Lord your God with all your heart and with
> all your soul and with all your mind and with
> all your strength.' The second is this: 'Love
> your neighbor as yourself.' There is no com-
> mandment greater than these" (verses 29-31).

Jesus said the "heaviest" law is this: Love God and
love others. This is where the journey back to Sinai
begins. We must teach our world to love God and
others.

Jesus' answer began with what the Hebrews
called the *Shema*. *Shema* is the Hebrew word for
"hear," the first word in the passage which says,
"Hear, O Israel: the LORD our God, the LORD is one.
Love the LORD your God with all your heart and with
all your soul and with all your strength" (Deuteronomy 6:4, 5). Every pious Jew started his day by
saying the Shema. And before he went to bed at
night, he said it again.

The Shema was highly revered by the Jews, so the first part of Jesus' answer probably did not surprise many people. But what Jesus added was astounding. To the Shema, he added a phrase, "Do not seek revenge or bear a grudge against one of your people, but love your neighbor as yourself. I am the LORD" (Leviticus 19:18). And God extends the idea to foreigners: "When an alien lives with you in your land, do not mistreat him. . . . Love him as yourself, for you were aliens in Egypt. I am the LORD your God" (Leviticus 19:33).

Why did Jesus give *two* answers when he was asked for the most important *one*? The reason, I believe, is that there is such a connection between the two that they are inseparable. It is *only* in showing our love for others that we show our love for God. If we can understand that connection, we will be at the very heart of the ethic God desires for his people of character. Jesus' answer has three clear implications.

1. The beginning point is not our love for God, but God's love for us. Scripture never starts with our response to God. Notice that Jesus said, "Hear, O Israel: The LORD *our* God, the LORD is one." God should be loved totally and completely because he made a covenant of love with his people. He entered into it when they were not even seeking to be chosen, when they did not deserve to be chosen. The only way to explain God's choosing is grace. In the same way, God is our God because he chose us. Mark it down, Exodus always comes before Sinai. Before God gave us an ethic, he rescued us from bondage. Grace always comes before law. God always approaches us in love first. As the song says, "Oh, how I love Jesus." Why? "Because he first loved me."

2. We respond to God's love with devotion. Devotion means to love God with all your heart, soul, mind, and strength. It means to be completely, totally, sacrificially devoted to God. That's what happens when you love someone—you delight to serve them. When you love someone, you delight to please them. So notice the distinction. God's love for us stems from grace. There is no way to explain God's love for you and me but grace. There is nothing about us that merits such incredible love. God's love for us stems from grace, but our love for God stems from gratitude. Living lives of character is our response to God's gracious love for us.

It's like the boy who was once tempted by his friends to pick some ripe cherries from a tree which his father had forbidden him to touch. "You don't need to be afraid," they said. "If your dad finds out that you took them, he's so kind that he wouldn't hurt you." The boy replied, "That's why I shouldn't touch them. I know that my dad wouldn't hurt me, my taking them would hurt my dad."

3. Our gratitude to God is expressed in love for others. To love God is to make whatever matters to God matter to us. And what matters to God is people. Notice how John puts all three of these principles in two verses. "This is love: not that we loved God, but that he loved us and sent his Son as an atoning sacrifice for our sins. Dear friends, since God so loved us, we also ought to love one another" (1 John 4:10, 11). Wait! Did you notice the curve John threw? We expect him to say, "Since God so loved us, we also ought to love God." But what the verse says is "Dear friends, since God so loved us, we also ought to love one another." It is in loving one another that we express our gratitude to God for his love.

The only way we can show that we cherish the love of God is by sharing it. The problem with most ethical systems is that they try to make people love their neighbor without loving God first. And it just doesn't work that way because neighbors aren't always very lovable. But when we can see those neighbors as God's children, it puts things in a different light. What we have to realize is that showing love to others is the only way we have of showing our love for God.

The only way we can show that we cherish the love of God is by sharing it.

I'm reminded of the story of a professor who was an "expert" in raising children, although he didn't have any of his own. Every time someone tried to discipline a child, he would say, "Remember, you must love the child, not punish him." He decided to expand his driveway one day, so he mixed a load of cement. Just as he finished smoothing it and putting the trowel away, a child ran right through the work he had done, ruining it all. The professor was so upset, he ran after the child, picked him up, put him over his knee, and was about to paddle him when someone said, "Remember, professor, you should love the child, not punish him." To which the professor replied, "I do love him in the abstract, but not in the concrete."

We can sing "what the world needs now is love" all we want, but the problem is, it's usually easier to love "the world" than the people in it. As Charles Schultz's cartoon dog Snoopy says, "I love mankind; it's people I can't stand." Of course, when things are going smoothly, when relationships maintain an acceptable balance of give and take, we can be as loving as the next guy. But what happens when a relationship becomes more give than take? What happens when your neighbor keeps forgetting to return the tools he borrows? What happens when the insensitive husband doesn't respond to the wife's efforts to rekindle their love? What happens when a co-worker makes a habit of riding on your coattails?

I will always put you last until I learn to put God first.

My point is this: If we try to love our neighbors as ourselves by ourselves, we won't have the energy or the desire to live by our standard. For the fact is, most people don't deserve that kind of love. The only way we are going to be able consistently to live a life of loving others as ourselves is to be motivated to do so by God's incredible love for us—a love which we don't deserve either. That's why God's ten principles begin with our relationship to God, then address our relationship to others. I will always put you last until I learn to put God first. These are not very complicated concepts to grasp, but if we can incorporate these principles into our lives, we'll have grasped the heart of God's ethic for his people.

Self-Deception

Jesus said, "All the Law and the Prophets hang on these two commandments" (Matthew 22:40). Look at what Paul says:

> Let no debt remain outstanding, except the continuing debt to love one another, for he who loves his fellowman has fulfilled the law. The commandments, "Do not commit adultery," "Do not murder," "Do not steal," "Do not covet," and whatever other commandment there may be,

are summed up in this one rule: "Love your
neighbor as yourself." Love does no harm to its
neighbor. Therefore love is the fulfillment of
the law (Romans 13:8-10).

That's the final word. Love is the fulfillment of the
law, which means that there are a lot of us who may
think we're walking by God's ethic but who, sadly,
are not. As the old cartoon character, Hambone,
used to say, "There ain't no use trying to talk to God
when you're not speaking to your neighbor."
Jesus gave two examples of this type of self-
deception. The first is found in Matthew 19. It's the
story of a rich young man who came to Jesus one day
with a pressing question. (This is the Rick Atchley
Paraphrase Version, by the way.) He asked Jesus,
"What good thing must I do to inherit eternal life?"
That's an important question, and Jesus gave him a
good answer. He said, "Keep the commandments."
"Which ones?" the young man asked.
Jesus said, "You know which ones. Don't covet;
don't steal; don't commit adultery; honor your father
and mother."
Now this young man had the audacity to say,
"Well, I've been doing that. No problem here. I keep
the Ten Commandments." I hope by now you see the
problem with his answer. God's ethic is not about
merely *avoiding evil*. It's about *doing good*. God
wants his people of character to develop a lifestyle of
authentically, creatively, and sacrificially loving the
people he has placed around them. And Jesus decided
it was time for this young man to learn that lesson.
"Okay," Jesus said, "if you want eternal life, here's
what you do. You've got a lot of stuff; you're a rich
man. You sell all your stuff and give it to poor people
who don't have anything. Then come follow me, and
you will have riches in heaven."

The Bible says the young man then went away sad
because he was very wealthy. He's the only person I
know of who sought out Jesus and left in worse
shape for his encounter.

The point of the story is that most people would
have pointed out the young man as an outstanding
example of keeping the law of Moses. Most people
would look at him and believe he was obedient and
moral. He was the kind of man most people would
want their daughters to marry. He seemed like a
man of character, but Jesus showed that despite the
young man's outward conformity to God's ethic, he
was *not* a person of character. His reaction to Jesus'
instructions exposed a love for something that was
greater than his love for others and even greater
than his love for God. He had deceived himself.

How Far Does It Go?

Our second example from Jesus' earthly ministry
is from Luke 10 (Rick Atchley Paraphrase, again). In
this encounter, a teacher of the law asks Jesus the
same question the rich young man asked: "What
must I do to inherit eternal life?" Jesus asks the
man, "What do you think?" And the teacher replies,
"Well, after years and years of reading the law, I
have determined that it all comes down to two
things; love God with all you have and love your
neighbor as yourself." Jesus said, "Right. Go do it."

*Love God with all you have and love
your neighbor as yourself.*

But then the man wanted to justify himself, so he
said, "Yes, but how far do you go with that neighbor
business? I mean, just exactly who is my neighbor,

and where do I draw the line?"

So Jesus said, "Let me tell you a story." We call it the story of the good Samaritan. I'll tell you now, though, that we don't appreciate this story the way Jesus' hearers did when he told it because the word *Samaritan* doesn't make us cringe and sweat and frown like it did them. Maybe if Jesus were telling this story today to white people in South Africa, the part of the Samaritan would be played by a member of the National African Congress. Or if he told it to the Catholics in Northern Ireland, it would be a British soldier. Perhaps if he told it to us, it would be a third-generation welfare recipient, a homeless person, or an HIV-positive homosexual.

Whoever it is you need to put in the place of the Samaritan to make this story shocking for you, do so, and we'll begin the story. It seems a fellow was going down to Jericho when robbers ambushed and waylaid him. They beat him, took his clothes, and left him half dead in a ditch. He didn't know what to do. They didn't have mobile phones back then, so he couldn't dial 911. He just lay there, bleeding and waiting, until he heard footsteps.

He looked up and saw the tassels on the robes of a priest, and his heart leapt within him. Help had arrived! But, no! The priest saw him all right, but he crossed to the other side of the road and went right on past.

The man let his head drop back to the ground. What would he do now? Perhaps the priest had been his last hope. Again, he heard footsteps. He looked up and saw the robes of a Levite—a worker in the church. Surely he would help! But the Levite also crossed the road and passed quickly by when he saw the injured man.

Surely, there was no hope now. The man lay down and prepared for death to come. But instead of dying, he heard a donkey. The man looked up in hope, but immediately sank back down. "Some Samaritan dog. So this is how it will end. The Samaritan will finish me off for sure." Just as the man expected, the Samaritan got off his donkey and approached. The man braced himself for the blows, but, instead, he felt the soothing cool of ointment on his gaping wounds. What is happening? the man thought. Can this be real?

The Samaritan put his hands under the man and picked him up. He laid him across his own donkey and led the way to the closest inn. The Samaritan cared for the wounded man, then he gave the innkeeper some money along with instructions to meet all the wounded man's needs. And he gave a promise that he would pay all the man's expenses when he returned.

Jesus' story illustrates the three ethics by which people live:

1. The robber's ethic—What's yours is mine, and I'll take it. A lot of people live this way. "You have something I don't. If I have to harm you to get what I want in life, I'll do it."

2. The priest's and Levite's ethic—What's mine is mine, and I'll keep it. This is how most people—sadly, even most religious people—live. "I'm not going to do you any harm, but I'm not going to do you any good either. I'm just going to take care of me."

3. The Samaritan's ethic—What's mine is yours, and I'll share it. People of character live this way. "God helps me, so let me help you."

Jesus turned to the teacher of the law and asked, "Which one of these men was a neighbor to the one in trouble?" And the teacher couldn't stand it. He didn't want to have to answer, but he finally spit out the words, "I guess the one who showed mercy." And

Jesus turned and said, "Go and do it."

Now why do you think Jesus went to such lengths to choose such an objectionable hero for his story? Why didn't he have the priest or the Levite or at least some poor Jewish peasant rescue the wounded man? He certainly could have chosen one of these, for Jesus' point was not that participating in organized religion automatically makes people hypocrites. But he chose someone that his audience would not associate with religion because he wanted to make the point that mere outward showings of allegiance to God are not enough to please him.

God expects from his people of character a love so overwhelming that it makes doing the unthinkable a way of life.

God expects from his people of character a love so overwhelming that it makes doing the unthinkable a way of life. Look at the story from the Samaritan's perspective. Do you think he had somehow remained unstained and unaffected by the racism and hatred between these two cultures? Yet when God placed a Jew in need of help in the Samaritan's path, there was no question in his mind, no hesitation in his hands, no holding back from the service to which God had called him. He had learned what the priest and Levite had not. He had come to accept that along the path to eternal life we encounter people who need help—people we are not to avoid or pass by while praying for their healing, but people *we* are to help. Like the Samaritan, God's people of character love him enough to love them. And in loving them, they love him.

Living lives of character means being willing to give up any source of security, any tradition, or any personal preference for the sake of the people in the ditch. The only way we can love God is to love what matters to God, and what matters to him are the people he created and those he wants to recreate.

How Far Are You Saved?

The story is told that a Hindu man from the highest caste in India attended a Christian worship assembly one day. He listened awhile to what the minister was saying, then he stood up and announced, "I understand that you Christians believe you are saved. I, too, am saved, but not by Jesus Christ. I am saved by the religion of my fathers."

Surprised by the interruption, the preacher tried to be diplomatic and said, "Sir, I'm glad you feel you're saved. We're going down to feed and clothe the poor [(considered by higher castes to be "untouchables")] after our service here. You are welcome to join us."

The Hindu gentleman thought for a moment, then rose again and replied, "Sir, I still insist that I am saved, but I am not saved that far."

God's people of character, though, *are* saved that far. Jesus' teaching proclaims without any doubt that love truly is his greatest commandment—greatest in scope and in importance. The quality of character that God desires requires more of us than just keeping a checklist of dos and don'ts. He requires of us the practical, everyday living out of love for God and for neighbor, because rules alone have never been enough to keep us from sin. We're not going to stop committing adultery just because we hear the minister telling us adultery is a sin. We're

not going to stop lying and stealing because the
minister says so either. It's only when our hearts are
so filled with love for the God who pulled *us* out of
the ditch that he will matter enough to us to live by
his ethic. Only then will our quest for character be
fruitful.

Remember the young teacher from Mark 12? He
responded to Jesus by saying,

> Well said, teacher, . . . You are right in saying
> that God is one and there is no other but him.
> To love him with all your heart, with all your
> understanding and with all your strength, and
> to love your neighbor as yourself is more impor-
> tant than all burnt offerings and sacrifices
> (verses 32, 33).

And the crowd gasped. A teacher of the law was
speaking. He was in the temple, the holiest spot on
the earth for a Jew. It was Passover week—the week
when they gave more sacrifices than any other time
of the year. And this teacher in the temple at the
Passover was saying, "Love fulfills the law. Love is
more important than all these offerings and sacrifices." His bold insight certainly made an impression
on Jesus. And it is the key to solving the character
deficit. Jesus looked at this teacher and said, "You
are not far from the kingdom of God."

So, how do we become people of character in a
world that has lost its standards? What will we
learn when we return to the summit?

His Principles Are the Path

Go back and look at the principles again: (1) Put
God first; (2) Take God as he is; (3) Respect what is
holy; (4) Seek rest with God; (5) Make your family a

priority; (6) Respect human life; (7) Keep marriage sacred; (8) Keep "things" in perspective; (9) Tell the truth; (10) Be content. These are absolute values that express God's nature, that express his character. They are standards that are not going to change. Instead, they will provide a firm foundation for life. They reveal for us just what it means to love God and love people. His solutions are truly a path to a life of character. We must never give up on them, regardless of our culture and regardless of the worldly cost.

His Amazing Grace Is the Motivation

Remember that God had to stoop down to reach for us when we were in the ditch, and Jesus left his comfort zone to rescue us when we didn't even know we were at risk. Their divine acts of kindness and grace should motivate us to search for and serve those unlovely and unlovable people God puts in our paths. The kind of grace God has given us is worthy of total, complete, and extravagant devotion on our part toward God. As the song says, "Were the whole realm of nature mine, that were a present far too small. Love so amazing, so divine demands my soul, my life, my all."

His Holy Spirit Is the Enabler

We can't live God's ethic without God. We can't do it on sheer grit and determination. We must allow God to do the work of recharactering in us. If we'll let him, God will write his law in our minds and put it in our hearts, as he promised.

When we surrender to Jesus Christ, confess his name, and are born again, God sends his Holy Spirit to live in us and to begin the recharactering process. The very first thing he does is to plant in us the most fundamental ingredient of a life of character—God's

love. Paul explains that "God has poured out his love
into our hearts by the Holy Spirit, whom he has
given us" (Romans 5:5b). I don't know exactly how
God recharacters a life, but I have seen people so
dramatically changed that God is the only way to
explain the transformation.

One of my favorite stories from William Barclay's
commentaries is of a fellow who had lived a wicked
life. He was an alcoholic and was such a slave to
drink that his home didn't even have furniture because each week he drank up his paycheck. But when
he found Jesus Christ, God's Spirit began to work in
his life so dramatically he seemed like a new person.
At the factory, his co-workers gave him a hard time
about being a Christian. "Oh come on," they said.
"Don't tell us you're buying into all those stories they
tell from the Bible? You don't really believe Jesus
turned water into wine, do you?" The man thought a
moment, then said, "All I know is, at my house he's
turned beer into furniture." He was being changed
from the inside out because he experienced the grace
of God. The angels must rejoice to witness such a
recharactering of one of God's children!

Face to Face

The clouds have disappeared around the mountain. The sun is shining brightly, reflecting the
glories of heaven off the peak that juts into the crisp,
blue sky. You are standing at the base of the
Almighty's mountain with your heart thundering in
your ears.

The Sinai Summit is still in session. God alone
waits at the top of his mountain, hoping that you
will come up to meet him face to face. Like Elijah,
you can hear him whisper gently, "What are you
doing here, my child?" And you must answer.

You can choose to rail at today's society and blame
it for failure to follow God's principles. You may feel
that you're alone in your fight against the great
character crisis that is seemingly destroying our
nation and world. You may even cry out for God to
rescue you from the war by letting you die because
you're tired, and you have lost your confidence in his
solutions.

God will refresh you, discouraged servant. He will
show you that you are not alone in the battle. Thousands of his people around the world are fighting
valiantly to recharacter the world through love,
according to his instructions.

Look at the world relief organizations that are
reaching out to feed the starving. Look at the hun-
dreds of shelters for the homeless that are comfort-
ing God's little ones on the streets. Look at the
clinics and churches that are counseling rocky
marriages to save them. Look at halfway houses and
hospitals that are helping addicts recover their
character and their hope. Look at Christians who
are sharing the Word of God around the world,
teaching again God's instructions for strong character. Oh, you are *not* alone!

A return to God's values can solve America's
character crisis. And many are ready to join you in
the journey back to the summit at Sinai. It's a journey that begins in your heart . . . and it begins today.
The Lord of grace and love is waiting to meet with
you there.

Focusing Your Faith

1. Imagine that you are on Mount Sinai with God, and he has asked you, "What are you doing here, my child?" How do you respond to him?

2. "Exodus always comes before Sinai . . . Grace always comes before law." Why is law without grace unable to produce people of real character?

3. How can you express your gratitude to God for his saving grace? Refer to 1 John 4:10, 11.

4. Think of five ways you can work God's ten teachings into your everyday conversations with your friends.

5. "God expects from his people of character a love so overwhelming that it makes doing the unthinkable a way of life." What "unthinkable" things do your neighbors see you doing for them?

6. If you were going to create a slogan to help "recharacter" America, what would it be? How would you show that the Spirit of God must be a part of the recharacering process?

7. "The only way we can show that we cherish the love of God is by sharing it." What are some ways you can do that?